# The Thousand Lives of Ursula Jones

*Between Lucerne and London, Music and Archaeology*

## Heinz Stalder

*Edited and translated by Joy Puritz*

ISBN: 9798406093597


PublishNation
www.publishnation.co.uk

# Contents

# Foreword

I have known Ursula Jones since 1965, and for ten wonderful years I worked by her side with the English Chamber Orchestra. It was a very courageous decision for Ursula to engage me at that time as a young artist in the dual roles of conductor and pianist. Our first tour together with the orchestra in 1966 took us straight into the Prague Spring Festival and, in the summer of that year, to Lucerne, Ursula's home town. Her father, Walter Strebi, was one of the founders of the Lucerne Music Festival in 1938, and was its president from 1953 to 1966. Until his death he remained its honorary president. In 1982 Ursula's mother, Maria (together with Philip and Ursula Jones), founded the Maria und Walter Strebi-Erni Stiftung, a trust that is dedicated to the promotion of the cultural life of the city and canton of Lucerne. Ursula thus came from a family very much associated with music and, since my first performance in Lucerne in 1966, she welcomed me not only to her house but into her family, and always treated me as one of them. I was a friend of Maria Strebi-Erni until her death at the great age of 107, and, to this day, I am very grateful to the whole family for their warm welcome. For a young artist like me, this was of immeasurable value at that time. Even now Ursula and I regularly cross paths, and each time it is a great joy to see her and to hear how passionate she still is as a champion of young artists, and how she is enriching the musical world. I hope that she will be granted many more active years in perfect health, and that we will see each other many more times.

*Daniel Barenboim, May 2017*

# Chapter 1

## *From Lord's Cricket Ground to Hamilton Terrace*

On an oval green there are eleven men in neatly ironed trousers, white shoes, white polo shirts and light beige, mostly sleeveless, v-necked pullovers. Then, somewhere else on the cordoned off pitch, there are two men in black trousers, half-length white coats, with indescribable hats on their heads. Although they look like them, they are not butchers having wandered by mistake from Smithfield Market onto Lord's Cricket Ground. They most certainly have something to do with the game, sometimes drawing attention to themselves with peculiar hand and arm gestures, and, if the elegant players feel too hot in the sun, by taking their pullovers and sticking them into the belts of their mostly over tight coats. In the middle of the oval green there is a narrow strip of worn grass. At both ends of the strip a man is standing, each in front of three vertical sticks over which the men in coats have, before the game, laid two little bits of wood horizontally. The two men have helmets on their heads, visors over their faces, and rather smart looking protective devices on their legs. Then a man on the field clenching a little red leather ball between thumb, index and middle fingers, having rubbed it shiny, suspiciously close to his crotch, takes a run-up towards the man at the far end of the brown grass strip who is staring at him while tapping the ground a couple of times with a handy wooden bat, about a meter long. And then here in England it starts to rain.

But then a cloudless summer sky magically turns the legendary Lord's Cricket Ground and its stadium, in the elegant London district of St John's Wood, into a cathedral fit for the noble sport, it being after all reverentially known as the Mecca of all cricket.

Cricket? Well, yes, cricket often plays a decisive role in many a biography of an Englishman or Englishwoman, also in the life of a Swiss woman who became British by marrying an English-

Welsh musician. The land, in this after all not cheap metropolis, must be of exorbitant value. Immense grandstands, a press centre looking like a spaceship, and the filigree pavilion for the exclusive members of the MCC, the Marylebone Cricket Club, surrounded by the meticulously tended oval green.

The school teams of Eton and Harrow meet here for their traditional One Day Match. In the past, when their parents, grandparents, siblings, aunts, uncles and cousins were not yet obliged to work, the cricket match between the elite schools was one of society's seasonal highlights, taking place on quite an ordinary weekday.

Extravagant picnics are still celebrated on the cosy smaller greens, in memory of more glorious times. Champagne glasses, fine porcelain and silver cutlery are taken from travelling baskets and arranged carefully and elegantly. Here and there a gentleman walks by in discreet grey morning dress, complete with matching top hat. One or two ladies might present themselves with a Victorian flower arrangement on a wide-brimmed hat. Overall, however, the scene is more casual than formal.

A Wing Commander of the Second World War feels obliged, with a rather stiff upper lip, to explain the importance of the game on the Lord's green, at least as well tended as that mundane Wimbledon down the road. The affable veteran of Her Majesty lost an eye in aerial combat and was a better cricketer than today's, who were obviously mollycoddled boys from the best, or at least good families of the land. If you weren't called up by the Royal Air Force, life, at least when there were still the colonies, was just one big party.

According to a formula proportionate to the uneventfulness of proceedings on the green, the champagne has been infiltrated by Guinness. Black Velvet. A somewhat alcoholic mist hangs over the stadium of the most English of all English sports. Between his nostalgic statements about better times, the Wing Commander pushes fresh strawberries into his mouth. He is reminded, while glancing with lustful eyes at scantily dressed young things, of Baudelaire's poem about the strawberry mouth and the fierce desire that overcomes him at the sight of red young lips. The match ends before tea and is declared a draw, after meticulous counting of fallen wickets, runs, overs and no balls. The old soldier's anecdotes: 'The older you get as an officer, the more you become an old soldier', begin to lack humour and to gain in lewdness.

Suzie Maeder, a photographer, although mostly involved in classical music, is working with a Swiss writer who is putting together a feature article about Lord's Cricket Ground for a Swiss newspaper. But Suzie cannot go into the shadowy secret Long Room in the pavilion (in 1992 women are still not allowed; only the Queen, being gender neutral, is allowed into the sacrosanct room); however, further down St John's Wood Road and into the dead straight Hamilton Terrace, Suzie has an acquaintance who, if she is at home, is good for a cup of tea, coffee or a glass of wine.

She is at home.

Through a well tended little front garden some steps lead up to a brown door with no number and an elegant Regency fanlight.

The lady of the house opens up, is pleasantly surprised, laughs, embraces the acquaintance, and introduces herself to the writer as Ursula Jones. She speaks with a pure Lucerne city dialect. In the corridor leading to her office, with the dining room on the left and then the kitchen, old engravings are hanging, drawings that look familiar, photos, framed concert flyers. The word 'brass' is often mentioned. One photo is of Wilhelm Furtwängler in bathing trunks. Next to him a handsome man dressed the same.

'My father,' Ursula explains.

Both the men loved the Lucerne Lido and were enthusiastic swimmers. Ursula's father was a famous sportsman, a sprinter, selected in 1924 for the Olympic Games in Paris for the 100 and 200 metres. A torn muscle prevented him from starting. Dr Walter Strebi: lawyer, co-founder of the Lucerne Festival, city councillor of Lucerne in charge of schools and the police. It is a long time ago: more than three-quarters of a century.

Ursula is an Englishwoman, a Londoner, at home here, rooted in Hamilton Terrace, where for a long time everyone knew everyone else as in a village and which was mostly occupied by artists and art lovers. But now, if someone sells up and moves away, because of age or because their house has become too large once the children have left, people arrive mainly because they can afford the house prices. The latter, almost daily, become ever more astronomical.

'Please come out into the garden. Under the big pear tree there's enough shade, but you can still get a bit of sun.'

The garden is narrow, in between overgrown walls over which one can get a feeling for the neighbours just by looking at the trees, even though one is unable to see them properly without standing on tiptoe or climbing up a ladder. Behind some more well kept trees and shrubs one can see the little house in which, in the past, the cart, horses and the coachman were housed. A car is in the garage. A Porsche. Not a status symbol. Absolutely not! Much more important are the two bicycles: a modern one for the lady, a genuine English old-timer for the gentleman. The occupant of the simple but not modestly furnished mews house is a single man, a gentleman through and through, a passionate admirer of Maria Callas. His collection of programmes, photos and write-ups is immense: many with very personal dedications. If one listened carefully, one might sometimes hear that great voice. Against a deep blue sky one can see and hear an aeroplane on its ascent from Heathrow. With a north wind one is also meant to be able to hear the storms of applause coming from the cricket stadium at Lord's. Apparently there have been visitors in Ursula's garden able to follow the results of the matches just by listening to them.

No, she does not understand the game. Once, when she was urgently in need of an extra trumpeter for the Philharmonia Orchestra performing Verdi's *Requiem*, and contacted a certain Philip Jones, she did not even know the difference between cricket and croquet, but then was rather shocked that this musician was turning down an engagement in favour of a cricket match. Well, that's the English for you: a bit quirky and of a different cultural ilk to artists of continental Europe. And yet it was of all people musicians, almost always working freelance, who relied on well paid engagements.

From the next house but one, a gentleman greets her, apologises, wants on no account to disturb her, only to let her know that he is home again and that everything has gone well.

Ursula thanks him and asks if he would like to come over for a quick glass of wine.

'Gladly,' says the gentleman, but in a quarter of an hour he would have to go to a meeting with the Philharmonia Orchetra.

'Sir Charles Mackerras', says Ursula, 'an Australian conductor who has worked for a long time in Europe, in Hamburg, Prague and now especially in London. One of the really great conductors, famous for his many services to music. Without him the Czech composer Janáček would probably have been forgotten.'

Then there is the story about a lodger in another neighbouring house who had been invited to a charity dinner, had a dark suit but no shirt fitting the dress code for the occasion. As the lodger was about the same size as Sir Charles, Ursula had the idea of asking Lady Mackerras if she could help out the man who was in this fix. Shortly afterwards the bell rang in the basement and a dainty lady was standing at the door with three shirts, a cummerbund and a black bow tie. At the charity event Sir Charles Mackerras conducted and Janet Baker sang. At the following dinner the lodger in a stranger's shirt discovered that the conveyer of the necessary items of clothing had been the wife of the famous conductor. He acknowledged her friendly wave with a shy nod, and Sir Charles stood up and boomed in his mighty bass voice, 'So you are the man in my shirt!' right across the room.

Ursula knows innumerable anecdotes, and there is no shortage of those in the world of musicians and singers. The cool white wine is South African; by now she knows how to do almost anything in the unfussy English way, such as magically producing snacks in this wonderful refuge in the middle of the busy, never resting city.

Lying on a little white garden table are two reddish-orange books that Ursula has been leafing through before the unexpected visit. As she notices the curious glances directed at them, she seems embarrassed, but allows them to be picked up, literally still smelling of fresh print. They are heavy. Volume 1: 700 grams, Volume 2: 1.7 kilos.

'Ursula Jones: Decorated Metates in Pre-Hispanic Lower Central America. University of London 1992.'

Ursula's brilliant doctorate about prehistoric grinding stones of Central America. And when she tries to qualify the justified astonishment at her achievement with her winning, honest smile, a bit of pride and satisfaction is there, thank goodness. On each of the volumes is a picture of a 'metate' (grinding stone) meticulously researched by Dr Jones: on the cover of Volume 1, one looking like an elongated concave table, carved and decorated in basalt, with a mano, a stone roller which was moved with both hands over the maize to be ground. On Volume 2 there is a metate in the form of a stylised and much decorated animal, probably a reptile. These milling utensils go back to the early centuries A.D. Ursula's research was concentrated on the region between Honduras and the present-day Panama Canal. In previous studies these decorated grinding stones were often described as altars, thrones, tables for cult ceremonies, and less often as metates. Ursula proves in her work that the majority of her findings, amongst over 650 specimens, suggest that these are first and foremost simply practical grinding stones, and that the more decorated ones were probably used for ritual milling. The fact that the production of flour, the basic substance for our daily bread, could also be part of mysticism and symbolism would make sense even to the most down-to-earth layman. An incredible work: four chapters with many subsections, with innumerable foot notes and sources, sketches and chronological particulars in the first volume; and in the second 650 objects, minutely annotated with geographical, geological facts, with particulars of mass and weight, and where they are now to be found. After the 303 pages of Volume 1 there are another 651.

How does a woman of 60 years land herself with such a hard task? It was her dream since childhood to dig for treasures of the past. 'Archaeology is rubbish,' her parents allegedly once said to one another, quite satisfied with their misunderstanding of the social science. Rubbish, useless stuff. Rubbish, yes: leftovers from the olden days, fragments from which the vanished whole can be deduced, which open our eyes to what is lost. But despite her urge to study the science, Ursula's assertions had failed.

Languages were in vogue after the war, if law was considered out of the question for a young woman. Those who could express themselves not only in German, but mastered Italian, French of course, and especially English, would find it easier to achieve something in life than by shuffling around ruins on their knees, digging for shards with little shovels and tiny brushes, like children in a sandpit, and perhaps happening upon an old coin. And then, if it proved to be valuable, they would certainly have no right of possession. So, after Middle School, a useful course of study had to be followed. Ursula obeyed, became a translator and then, thanks to her father's many connections, was also soon at home in music promotion. The languages helped her with the often very trying organising of musicians, orchestras, concerts and tours.

After many years in the music business, so many different factors were involved that, despite her usual optimistic enthusiasm, she began to be disillusioned by certain things. With her unconditional support for her husband Philip, she not only began to yearn after her earlier career dreams, she applied herself more to realising them, joined students on the hard benches in lecture halls and immersed herself in a subject which, with every lecture, began to fascinate her more and more.

Despite this new occupation and great challenge, music was not cast aside. The Philip Jones Brass Ensemble continued to gain a good reputation; the critics and connoisseurs agreed: here was a man who countered the negative side of brass music by inspiring outstanding arrangements of the classics. Ursula's experience as a manager contributed considerably to the ensemble's reputation.

That Mrs Jones should occupy herself with only one thing was unthinkable, even in those days. Over there in the mews, in the neat coach house where Philip Jones' mother had lived, there was also the garage. Musicians work at night, students often as well. The clicking of Ursula's shoes from the garage to the house and back again, this nocturnal, constant back and forth in the silent nights of the peaceful backs of Hamilton Terrace would not have been heard over long distances. Yet the Shell director who lived next door found it disturbing. 'Mrs Jones!' he loudly addressed her, frightening her to death on her way from her job to her archaeology and back again to her music, 'when are you going to change your impossible way of life?'

It is possible that Ursula's instantly quieter gait allowed the disobliging neighbour to sleep even less soundly.

Her title of doctor and the subsequent teaching undoubtedly changed her life and accelerated her rhythm through several cadences. The preparation of her first lectures was so meticulous and polished to the finest detail that she never got around to reflecting upon them, waiting for feedback and practising quality control. Her constantly cheerful, never aggressive or arrogant attitude to others encouraged her first students at an adult education college to point out to her that a little less subject matter would be decidedly better.

'I wanted to pass on all my knowledge, stored in an already somewhat aged brain and then adapted for a student course. I had to bear in mind that, as a newcomer, there might be some gaps in my knowledge.'

Her laugh is hearty: a summer laugh. Somewhere high up in the sky over London a bird seems to be joining in. As soon as interest in her as a person, in her extraordinary life and work, reaches a critical level, she gets an alarm signal that makes her retreat into her undeniable modesty. But is she not somewhat proud of all she has achieved, due to her talent and indefatigable graft?

'A little bit. Maybe.'

'How was the cricket match at Lord's?' she asks, leading the conversation in another direction. She asks herself how this miracle could have occurred: that she, someone from the continent, is suddenly interested in a sport that one would normally have had to grow up with in order to have an inkling as to what was happening on that oval field, that is if it did not start raining.

There is not enough time to pass on the knowledge gained at Lord's by this lady who has travelled the world with her English Chamber Orchestra, and paved the way to Mount Olympus for her best musicians.

In the office, through which one reaches the garden, the phone is ringing yet again. There is no answerphone. Ursula does not want to be tied down by constant contactability, and be at everyone's beck and call. Anyone who has something important to say, to ask or to reply to, should phone again. It is bad enough with the computer and all those impersonal e-mails robbing one of time when one could be conducting personal conversations. In the corridor leading to the front door she does after all pick up and says her telephone number with incredible speed. A person's name is then called out in delight. The visitors wait, look with awe at more pictures and photos. Some are very familiar. Toscanini is unmistakable, pictured together with Ursula's father too.

The man on the phone is inviting Ursula to the Clonter Opera.

'Would you like to come? Near Manchester. My sister-in-law lives in Ollerton. The house is big enough. Marah would be glad to put us up.'

# Chapter 2

## *The Ernis of Winkelried*

One of the musicians whom Ursula discovered, promoted and looked after, will one day say that without her, after his training was completed, he would have had to look for a position as a music teacher, and would have moved far away into the provinces, put down roots and, to the end of his days, led the humble life of a moderately talented person bereft of all his dreams. At the beginning of his career Duncan Ward was Sir Simon Rattle's assistant for the Berlin Philharmonic.

And she? What was her start in life like? Ursula looks out through the railway carriage window at the English Midlands.

In the late 1930s Lucerne looked a bit different from this gentle landscape divided by hedgerows under a sky that, over the meadows, woods, single houses, the villages with their typical church towers, the mansions, stately homes and castles, spreads a light that hardly anywhere has such a magical effect as here, on the island of Her Majesty the Queen; even though, for quite some time now, the cooling towers of a nuclear power station are to be seen, and in the smaller towns the suburbs and roads to the railway stations look rather duller than elsewhere.

An extremely happy childhood is not how she would describe hers. Her mother liked moving house constantly, to find something better, and probably also so as to be able to move in correspondingly better social circles. The parents did not spend much time on little Ursula. There was always something more sensible, more important, more profitable to do and to plan, than to bring up a daughter who soon brought her lack of upbringing to fruition, extended the various phases at her defiant stage as the mood took her, and rebelled.

Luckily for the unruly but always cheerful girl there were any number of uncles and aunts on her mother's side who were glad to make time, or perhaps had to, to occupy themselves with the little, inquisitive, enterprising and attention-seeking Ursula.

Even today, if a load-bearing vehicle bumps and clatters over rough ground, streets, town squares or rail lines, she recalls the pleasure of the times when her uncles would give her rides on a serving trolley on the Bireggstrasse in Lucerne. The to-and-fro of the clanking wheels of the unstable vehicle, together with Ursula's squeals of delight and the boyish laughter of the men, grew so loud that even the horses of the horse trader Kaufmann on the other side of the street joined in with their whinnying.

Aunt Griti became Ursula's admired and beloved substitute mother. She made time, always had time, played with her, told her stories, which Ursula can no longer remember in detail, but which are so deeply rooted in her whole being that images of perfect beauty are conjured up whenever she hears the name Griti.

By contrast, not all the celebrities who visited the Strebi-Erni house during the weeks of the International Music Festival quite passed muster. Already as a child Ursula was exceptionally good at judging people. Beautiful people fascinated her, as long as their looks were matched by the inner values she demanded.

Father Walter Strebi was an athletically built, extremely attractive man. Mother Maria placed much value on superficialities, but also excelled in matters of business, was an intrepid fighter for women's rights, loved art, was a great reader, and understood more about music than some of her illustrious guests. With their small talk they were on a level far below the flexible eloquence of their hostess.

Ursula inherited much from her mother in the way of ideals. On the material side, however, she was disinherited by her parents, who had a considerable fortune at their disposal when she married Philip Jones; and she put her signature to a renouncement of the statutory minimum portion. Music, yes, but not a musician as a husband: an Englishman, a trumpeter, an artist who would be like a hawker having to show his licence in order to be allowed to perform.

Aunt Griti loved walks along the Schweizerhofquai in Lucerne, and little Ursula was quite happy among the people, the elegant ladies and the always rather stiffer gentlemen with walking sticks; she had fun looking out for particular extravagances, would laugh, but not at them. The rather quirky English people especially did it for her. She could not understand their language, but recognised it by the sounds of the words, by the discreet gestures, the consciously played-down arrogance, by the stiff upper lips and the attire, which in masterly fashion distinguished itself from off-the-peg clothing. Not to mention the ladies' hats. Already very early on there must have been an affinity, a fascination, although a critical one.

'I winked at them, did an almost imperceptible curtsey, and the "Englishly" elegant ladies, gentlemen, lords and dames on their by now almost ritualistic promenade before dinner, nodded back at the little madam: some taken aback and rather awkward, others amused, astonished. The rest foresaw perhaps that one day in Buckingham Palace I would be named, by Her Majesty the Queen, Officer of the Order of the British Empire.'

The fellow passengers on the train to Manchester turn round at the sound of the hearty, loud, but not too loud, laughter. The looks are not angry. Perhaps they have understood that a foreign subject of the Queen has just remembered an amusing occurrence at court.

Yes, there are plenty of those: anecdotes from the circles of illustrious nobles. The King of Tonga was on a state visit to England, and because the exotic Royal Highness had seen and heard the royal brass band, he decided to draw up such a formation too and to make his parades more spectacular. With this in mind Ursula and Philip Jones were invited to a private luncheon at Buckingham Palace in order to give advice and support to the King of Tonga on the subject. Philip was always convinced that the Queen had been obliged, at the request of her royal guest, to order a search through the Yellow Pages for a connoisseur in matters of brass music. When Ursula mentioned to one or two friends that she and Philip had been invited to lunch at Buckingham Palace with the King of Tonga, she was often told of an amusing occurrence that took place during the coronation celebrations for Elizabeth II: a friend of the flamboyant writer and actor Noël Coward is supposed to have asked, as the open coach with the Queen of Tonga went by, who the small man dressed in white was next to the very sturdily built lady. 'Her lunch', Noël Coward is supposed to have replied, without batting an eyelid. At the lunch at Buckingham Palace the King of Tonga was late, and during a relaxed conversation the anecdote came up again, although the Queen attributed the disrespectful answer to Winston Churchill, whereupon Ursula spontaneously corrected Her Majesty and declared Noël Coward the originator. Ursula's cheek in correcting the Queen made Philip want the ground to swallow him up.

Apropos of putting one's foot in it: Ursula's other aunt, the great but unassuming art collector and patron, Berthe Kofler, like all the Ernis a highly talented painter herself, had put on a private exhibition of her works. On this occasion a friend of Ursula got into conversation with a lady who was equally keen on art and talked excitedly about these works of the sister of Hans Erni, whom every child had heard of. He said that if he wanted to be absolutely honest, he would take his hat off to this unknown sister rather than to her big brother, who was much too popular, much too decorative. Someone who knew the Erni family well, elbowed Ursula's friend in the ribs. The lady he was talking to so knowledgeably was no other than Doris, Hans Erni's wife, the brilliant saleswoman and promoter of that creator of distinctive horses and gracefully flowing human bodies.

Ursula liked being in Uncle Hans's studio when she was a child. He was also a great wordsmith. In Winkelriedstrasse, where the Ernis lived in Lucerne, he initiated his little niece in the family secret, never to be divulged to anyone else: that the Government had discovered in ancient documents that they were the Ernis of Winkelried, who had been ordered on the highest authority and befitting their social status, to move to the street of their name. Ursula believed everything this man said; a man, moreover her uncle, who knew how to express himself far better than the average of her acquaintances and relatives, could paint and draw, could say more with a brush- or pencil-stroke than her father (who, being a lawyer, had not exactly fallen flat on his face either). Well, she believed almost everything. Some things sounded too neat and clever to be true, to hold up through thick and thin. His Communist beliefs might have been temporary, but

13

his political conviction made the girl hang on his every word, and seems to have made more of an impression than her parents might have been happy about, being firmly at the other end of the political spectrum.

During the Second World War, when Walter Strebi, as a lawyer, began to worry about the possible reduction of potential clients affecting his usual standard of living, he switched temporarily to politics, became a liberal city councillor of Lucerne, in charge of schools and the police: N.B. with a daughter who caused nothing but trouble at school, often having to stand outside the door due to chatting in class. Outside in the corridor she would always carve her initials 'US' with the day's date into the wall with the clothes pegs, above the shoe racks and benches. When, doubtless influenced by Uncle Hans, she finally wrote 'Love Daddy Stalin' in large letters in thick chalk on the blackboard, both her parents were summoned to the school. Naturally it was more than a little embarrassing for the liberal city councillor to be confronted with the misdemeanour of his communist daughter, but he dared not show any sign of weakness. If this child, quite obviously led astray, did not markedly improve, she would be threatened with admission to a notorious reform school.

Nevertheless, Ursula spent the summer holidays in Lehn, the urban holiday home near Eigenthal, high above Kriens. Her mother led the child on foot from Kriens via the countless flights of steps of the pilgrims' path up to the pilgrimage church in the Hergiswald, and the same distance again, steeply and high up into the chapel, the Holderchäppeli, and the big house. From there one of the loveliest views of the city of Lucerne was awe-inspiring. Her parents had placed Ursula up there, more or less in sight and yet so very far away, in order to be rid of her for a whole summer, yet it did not make the child less problematic, even though she occasionally missed home. One had to shower once a week, in one's swimming costume. Yet up there in Lehn, a bit nearer to the sky than in Lucerne, the city of light, there were other children who were mostly cheerful and in the mood for some fun, if they were not actually weeping homesick tears. Above all there was no housekeeper who, at the slightest wrongdoing, could grab the carpet beater and, with the full permission of the parents, give a good hiding with her elongated hand.

Things were critical for Ursula when one evening she took advantage of her parents' absence for a rendezvous with a boyfriend. She helped herself from her fashion-conscious mother's wardrobe, put on an expensive fur jacket and climbed out of the window. As chance would have it, her parents, who normally never came back from their social engagements before midnight, had forgotten something and soon returned home to find that Ursula had flown the nest, not returning until late at night, flushed with excitement. Nothing, absolutely nothing immoral had happened in those few hours with the boy, who was the same age as she was, and really quite shy. Wearing her mother's fur jacket she was caught in flagrante delicto. Father's lawyer's German was mixed with words that could have grown on the dung heaps of the hinterland rather than in the offices of Lucerne.

Reluctantly, Ursula can still remember the argument that seemed to go on forever, and has perhaps, after more than 70 years, repressed and forgotten some of it. But she remembers exactly how, on every bit of her linen and clothing, she had to sew those horrible tapes with exactly the same initials as she had previously carved into the wall of the school corridor. Every stitch pierced her heart. Oh yes, in her late 80s she still feels the stitches just as much as all those years ago.

'Guilty children's clothes had to have nametapes. My father must have known that. It could be that my mother agreed out of fear of a drastic punishment: that I, in that seductive fur jacket, might have tempted and incited the young boy to do something that would have brought social disgrace and ostracism upon the family.'

To support more rights for women was something quite different from teaching a pubescent daughter the facts of life. She was not sent to an approved school. Although there was no gutter press yet in the late 1940s, there would almost certainly have been a full-blown scandal, had the affair had consequences. Had the daughter of a local city councillor, in charge of schools and the police and a founder of the music festival, been brought up in an institution of brutal strictness, it would have shaken Lucerne's society more deeply than the desecration of the Lion of Lucerne monument or a concert of carnival music in the Jesuit church.

Was it all perhaps just a hard threat, a screen drawn across a failed upbringing, the sewing on of initials a broad hint? One of the things that she has not come to terms with is that she can today, as perhaps then, laugh about the reaction of her parents, unable to cope with their daughter's puberty; the other: that that failure of her parents sometimes still makes her sad.

Ursula experienced the saddest moment in all her young days on the steps of the Reformed Lukaskirche (Church of St Luke) in Lucerne. Aunt Griti, whom she admired above anyone else and by whom she was equally loved, had just got married in the church, had said goodbye and was now going away forever with her husband, away from Lucerne, far away over the hills to the canton of Zurich: to a farm in Horgen Oberdorf. America could not have been worse or so final. Ursula had to understand that Aunt Griti could never again be hers alone. Though she liked the man whom Aunt Griti followed in her bridal gown, no one had dared to tell Ursula what she already knew: that the woman, who meant far more to her than her mother, would from now on always be smiling at this farmer from Horgen Oberdorf. Gone were the walks; no more curtseying to flamboyant Englishmen, never again having the feeling that she was living in the same world as these people from this great wide world full of secret islands, to which one had to travel on ships in comparison to which the paddle steamers on Lake Lucerne must look like little boats made of folded newspaper. And then, shocked awake out of dreams and Aunt Griti's stories, the rasping voice of the housekeeper, the horrible sound of a carpet beater whistling down onto her body. Her mother would never be capable of giving her the same feeling of security and adventure as Aunt Griti had done. Never was her mother more estranged from Ursula as then, as on the steps of the Lukaskirche when her world ended in a flood of tears. Waving, the wedding party said farewell to the wedded couple, and no one noticed Ursula's calamity. For the first time in her life Ursula was deeply unhappy.

As a dubious substitute for Aunt Griti a whole new world opened up for Ursula. After the concerts of the International Music Festival, the great artists, the contemporary composers and conductors were in and out of her parents' house. As the musical duo Marthely Mummenthaler/Vrenely Pfyl succinctly put it, in quite a different musical style:

'Wänns dr ganz Tag au schüüli grägnet het,
so als es nümme höre wett,
chunnt am Abig ganz verstohle d Sunne uf,
seit gueten Abig no im Bett.
Nach em Räge schiint Sunne,
nach em Briegge wird glacht.'

When it has poured with rain all day
As if it would never stop,
The sun furtively creeps out at evening
And says "good evening" while still in bed.
After the rain, comes the sun.
After crying, comes laughter.

Ursula still has a lot of time for folk music. Not so much for pop songs, with their hackneyed and often brash texts. If it is genuine and truly traditional, she has nothing against a rousing Ländler, a happy cheer; and when, in front of their chalet near Grächen, Philip Jones swapped his trumpet for the alphorn, sometimes accompanied by Ursula on her little accordion, her Schwyzerörgeli, it was always pure sunshine.

In Lucerne Ursula got used to the celebrities who turned the international music festival, co-founded by her father, into a great cultural institution, and the somewhat kitschy city of lights into a city of music. Ursula grew up with many highlights of classical and, thanks to the many works commissioned by the conductor and impresario Paul Sacher, modern music. She remembers with amusement that she could be disappointed when the perfection with which conductors and artists performed the music of Mozart, Haydn, Beethoven, Bach and Brahms, was not matched by their looks, as she would have expected. When these artists were invited to dinner by Walter and Maria Strebi, she, the bolshie wild animal with a latent tendency towards rebelliousness, was requested to dress herself suitably and not to shame her parents in any way. That was if she was allowed to bathe in the glow of the great stars in the first place.

When one evening her mother announced the famous composer Strauss, her disappointment was twofold. The already somewhat elderly and, according to Ursula's aesthetic expectations, not very attractive man, replied to her polite remark that she loved to hear *The Blue Danube* above all else, that unfortunately he was not Johann but Richard Strauss. Had she known then that this very same Richard Strauss thought of Giuseppe Verdi as little more than a composer of music for organ grinders, she would have let her childishly righteous anger pour all over the old blasphemer.

'Furti is coming, make the bed and don't forget the bolster!' rang through the house, if Wilhelm Furtwängler was coming and staying the night too. 'Furtwängler's long neck had to be made comfortable in a very special way.'

And then Ursula was overjoyed to discover that it was only a stone's throw over the Albis mountain range to Lake Zurich and Horgen Oberdorf. The farmhouse into which Aunt Griti had married was a little paradise. There was the farmhand, Fritz, who let Ursula climb up on the tractor beside him and chug across the seemingly vast meadows and fields. The land of her aunt and her husband seemed to her even vaster when she had to carry the basket with the afternoon picnic over the meadows and fields on foot. The bread, the cheese, the occasional bacon and the cider left an unforgettable taste in her mouth and memory.

Every now and then Grandfather Erni came to visit. He was the engineer of a Lake Lucerne paddle steamer, and smoked the twisted cigars from Brissago, probably not only during his time off. Occasionally Ursula was allowed a single puff from the moist end of the burning stalk. Whether she liked the taste she can no longer remember, but the fragrance of the smoke, smelling of Ticino and Maroni, from the unusually shaped cigar with a mouthpiece made of straw, remained in her memory.

Ursula was for many years herself a heavy smoker of Gauloises Bleues. While she was managing a large part of London musical life, together with Mansel Bebb (later to become the legendary manager of the Philharmonia Orchestra), in the basement of her house in Hamilton Terrace, smoke is supposed to have billowed out of the window as if the laundry of the whole of Paddington were being boiled there.

Her grandfather had a striking personality: a figure of a man straight out of an exclusive picture book. His beard was legendary. He was dressed like an Englishman: a reminder of the strolling tourists on the Schweizerhofquai. Much later Ursula discovered that her grandfather (who never made it to captain of a paddle steamer) was the image of the great Irish dramatist George Bernard Shaw. 'Without my grandfather's double, there would never have been the play *Pygmalion* nor the musical *My Fair Lady*.'

Nevertheless, Grandfather Erni made sure throughout his whole life, on the almost equally famous route Lucerne-Weggis-Vitznau, that the powerful engines of the paddle steamers functioned just as reliably as Shaw's plays in the great theatres of the world. Ursula often went with her grandfather on the route from Lucerne via Weggis to Vitznau and back again, standing at the barrier next to the gleaming jumble of swinging drive shafts above which stood the little oil cans. The engineer had to check and top them up from time to time. On every journey, the fact that this imposing, good-looking man, without whom the paddle wheels would not turn at all, was her grandfather, filled Ursula with an indescribable feeling of happiness. The music of the mighty but oh so quiet oscillations of the untiring machine, the occasional hissing of the steam valves, the mystical swishing of the driving wheels, the Babylonic murmuring of the marvelling passengers, the announcements of the calling points, the sound of the steam hooter, like a brass ensemble with lots of tubas, made a lasting impression. To this very day these past images form a jigsaw puzzle made up of endless pieces.

Ursula had been at the hub of music long enough to know how to keep an orchestra going: occasionally, or sometimes regularly, it needed the engineer with the oil can, so that the conductor on the podium, like the captain on the bridge, could give the beat, determine the rhythm, and ensure against serious abuse of the score. And what meaning does a score have for a ship?

The plans of a shipbuilder, the marriage of seaworthiness with machinery right up to the signal horn on the funnel. At the first performance of the Philip Jones Brass Ensemble at the International Music Festival in Lucerne, everything nautical, rhythmic and musical seemed to come together to form an image of Ursula's childhood, to form a complete work of art. Even more so when, after the concert, enthusiastically received by the audience, Philip Jones and his band played an encore, letting rip the folksong 'Vo Luzärn gäge Wäggis zue' ('From Lucerne to Weggis'), arranged by his colleague and best friend, Elgar Howarth.

Grandfather Erni was an artist too. If he had not been too modest and assumed that the cobbler has to stick to his metier and an inland boatman to his short journeys, tools and oil cans, then his son Hans, Ursula's uncle, would not have found it so easy to follow in his footsteps along the steep career path up to his 100th birthday, often jealously mocked by other artists.

In Winkelriedstrasse, named 'by order of the Government', Grandfather had set up a workshop in his attic: a proper studio. Up there under the roof he stood, undisturbed by the swell of the lake, both feet planted in quite another world, and created in miniature for his grandchildren anything he might have dreamt of. Out of the most varied materials he created tiny houses, kitchens, bathrooms, living rooms with a library, bedrooms with a boudoir: functional to the last detail. One could open and close the doors and windows with tiny handles, the furniture separately made, and made to measure. Everywhere light switches. Whether lights came on when you flicked them, Ursula can no longer remember. It would not surprise her if they had. Those not in the know might have called these architectural works of wonder doll's houses. There was not a single grocer's shop in the whole town as perfect as the one Grandfather made. Mechanical toys were created. Ballerinas danced, gymnasts swung on horizontal and parallel bars. Aeroplanes circled on almost invisible wires. The minutely constructed paddle steamer, however, sank on launching. A circus under a real big top invited one to sensations on the trapeze and the high wire. Clowns made an imaginary audience laugh, animal trainers whipped lions, tigers, seals, horses and elephants around the arena. The circus parade left nothing to the imagination. Behind the windows of the circus caravans, barred for secrecy, exciting things were happening. Had he lived a few more years he would have managed to make a perpetuum mobile.

The eldest son of Grandmother Erni, Ursula's Götti Toni (Godfather Toni), was a kindly oddball. He smoked like a Turk, sometimes like the funnel of Grandfather's ship at full steam ahead.

During Ursula's not so glorious Gauloises time one could have bet on her having inherited the Erni genes, which tended to depravity, rather than the artistic ones. Philip Jones suffered from his wife's addiction. If he wanted to get out of his instrument what Handel had composed for the trumpet, he needed clean, fresh air, not air impregnated with nicotine and tar. Every one of Ursula's deeply inhaled cigarettes could have been a divorcing issue. Whether Philip's threats were really serious, Ursula did not want to know.

Mansel Bebb did not give up smoking. If someone asked after Mansel in the Festival Hall on the South Bank, the home of the Philharmonia Orchestra, they only had to follow the smoke that he left behind him in the corridors of the large building: in the end everyone managed to find the burning cigarillo.

Götti Toni, was supposedly also a chain smoker. He never grew old, literally puffing himself to death. In his room in the Erni residence in Winkelriedstrasse, the greatest variety of implements for beating or stabbing built up into a jumbled, terrifying collection of murder weapons. No, Ursula's godfather was not the slightest bit violent: he was peace-loving, almost gentle. Well, so what. Perhaps after all it was not just a fantasy of the most famous Erni, that they were directly descended from the hero of Sempach.

As far as he was concerned, Hans Erni was a convinced pacifist and felt nothing but revulsion towards weapons. That his older brother set up for himself a torture chamber, a 'museum' with spears, spikes, halberds, battle-axes, flails, Katzbalger swords, one- and two-handed swords, which little Ursula found less disturbing than the other family members did, must have gone very much against the grain. Did he perhaps invent the tale of the Ernis of Winkelried in order to take the sting out of the gruesome obsession of his brother? Thus he could dismiss the collection as an uninteresting arsenal, a junk room belonging to the sort of people who set themselves up as heroes, piling hostile spears onto an inflated ego.

Hans Erni's famous poster about the decline of forests, the gruesome, gaping wound in the neck of a humanised tree, remained more rooted in Ursula's memory than most of the other works of her extremely successful artist uncle. Ursula will not allow a word to be said against Hans Erni's graphic works.

Every Saturday Ursula's grandmother invited her children to supper. They often had 'Schnitz und Härdöpfel', made with pears and potatoes. Ursula, as the oldest of the next generation, was also invited. But her parents preferred to avoid these Saturday family get-togethers.

So that Grandmother should for once have the pleasure of flying, the family later gave her the present of a flight to London, where Ursula managed to take her to see the ballet, *Swan Lake*, from the Royal Box of the Royal Opera House, Covent Garden. (A former girlfriend of Philip's worked at Buckingham Palace, so he and Ursula had access to the box when it was available.) Her grandmother enjoyed the city to the full. Her only problem was with the escalators in the underground and, after returning home, wrote to Ursula that she had discovered to her great satisfaction that there was now such a contraption in the Lucerne department store, Nordmann, and that she would practise on it before her next visit to London.

# Chapter 3

## *The Abduction into the Turkish Bath*

At Clonter Opera in Cheshire the scene is set for a medley from Gilbert and Sullivan's comic operetta *The Gondoliers*: a story of love and confusion; a most enjoyable affair with melodies that even the dumbest of listeners would think they could render: a score full of catchy tunes. Ursula knows the artistic director of the rural opera house. However, Clonter cannot be compared to the renowned Glyndebourne.

On his estate in Glyndebourne, John Christie built for his wife, the singer Audrey Mildmay, a true opera house. At its opening in 1934, Fritz Busch conducted Mozart's opera *The Marriage of Figaro*.

Jeffrey Lockett began in Clonter with a charity concert. He arranged his barn in such a way that the ubiquitous straw bales could be piled up as rows of seats. In time the straw gave way to more comfortable seating arrangements, and the Clonter Farm Music Trust, with its exemplary educational inclination, and no longer merely smiled at, gained a reputation which many urban music colleges envy. *The Gondoliers* was at any rate more refreshing than those often rather dusty, boundlessly expensive productions of too familiar works in the distant, over large and often presumptuous London.

On being asked where *The Gondoliers* was premièred, that typical beaming, infectious smile passes over Ursula's face.

'In London, in The Savoy Theatre, on the Strand. On the road from Trafalgar Square to Fleet Street.'

This street Ursula knows from her experience as a passionate cyclist. A friend from her student days, after a first-rate gastronomic career, became the general manager of the Savoy Hotel. For a while Ursula had piano lessons at the City Lit, an adult education college in London. After lessons she would cycle down Keeley Street via Covent Garden to the Strand and, at the Savoy Theatre, turn into the only street in London with driving on the right, leading to the legendary Savoy. A liveried porter took charge of Ursula's bike as if it were a Rolls-Royce or a Bentley, another hotel servant led 'the best friend of the general manager' past the illustrious guests to lunch, to tea or dinner, according to the time of day, to Herbert Striessnig, the most charming Austrian in London for many years. The fact that the Savoy lost a lot of its charisma after his retirement is due to the incomparably discreet cordiality of Herbert Striessnig. And perhaps no porter ever again took charge of the bicycle of a grateful lady as if it were a piece of jewellery, and handed it back as if it were a royal carriage, after a certain length of time which, by order of the general manager, was never to be noted.

Already before the hotel, with its exclusive guest list of The British Empire, was built on the bank of the Thames by the owner of the Savoy Theatre, the première of *The Gondoliers* took place in that very theatre. Gilbert and Sullivan were anything but convinced royalists and had hardly anything in common with the affected behaviour of the Victorians. But to criticise the monarchy was a dangerous game, however vivacious and popular the melodies might be, and however cheerfully they were sung by the subjects of Her Majesty. In order to steer clear of difficulties arising from attacks on the royal court, the plots were made to take place far from England: in Venice and the fictitious Barataria. Then monstrosities such as 'the monarchy has been remodelled on republican principles' or 'when everyone is somebody, then no one's anybody' could be sung with impunity.

Ursula became an Englishwoman through marriage, but equally irrefutably she remained a one-hundred-per-cent committed direct democracy republican. Uncle Hans would certainly have been hugely disappointed if an Erni of Winkelried had gone over to the monarchists.

Ursula's mother was, during her long life, an inexorable fighter for equal rights and status for women. When Ursula was nationalised English, had sworn on a white Bible to serve Queen and country loyally, her mother at first thought this disloyal to Switzerland; on the other hand, her daughter had gained the right which Swiss men, in their unbelievable arrogance, denied her. When Ursula went to vote for her member of Parliament for the first time, she had to describe every last detail: how it had felt, what the voting papers looked like, whether they had to have a cross or one's whole name, out of how many candidates she was allowed to choose, how the count was done in order that everything was conducted with absolute security and correctly in every way, and was properly checked, how long it took before the results were announced. One could see that her mother was as envious of her daughter's rights as she was proud to be the mother of a daughter with the right to vote.

'She could just have asked Father,' reckoned Ursula.

But her mother wanted to hear it from a woman, not from one of those men who might keep some things under their hats. It was really true, the claim that was made, or rather sung, in *The Gondoliers*: when every woman is somebody, then not one is just anybody. That it might not be so different for men was to Maria Strebi of no account. The Commercial School for Girls in Lucerne was the first significant step into the emancipation for which Maria Strebi-Erni had lived for 107 years. The lack of consideration and affection for her daughter, Ursula, was the price she paid for her social and financial success.

Her daughter also attended the Commercial School for Girls, the 'elite training ground' for young women in Lucerne, and there appeared not to have been any disciplinary or other school difficulties in this institution. The nonconformist Ursula had found her way or had come to terms with things as they were. Had that anybody perhaps become a somebody?

Ursula is well aware that she, as the daughter of Walter and Maria Strebi, was from childhood familiar with the internationally best known musicians and artists, and with her innate charm and winning way made friends for life, was privileged, profited from 'connections' as, being an Englishwoman, she was now entitled to call them in English. But that all this made her into something special, she vehemently denies.

The chief memory of her, held by her fellow students from the commercial school, whom she took around London instead of organising an ordinary get-together, is of Ursula being kind, ready for anything out of the ordinary, for any adventure, but also ready to give the slightest bit of help. When asked about the out of the ordinary things, the adventures and her selflessness, they all laugh, look at one another and all agree: 'It's just Ursula. The same Ursula, who one day gets us the best seats in the opera house, who knows the South Bank as well as her house in Hamilton Terrace, mingles with celebrities, knows every woman and every man in the Wigmore Hall, who seems practically to own the most original restaurants and is greeted by the staff as their beloved regular, who personally knows stage actors as well as the jazz-players at Ronnie Scott's, who at Glyndebourne reserves for us a grand space for the interval picnic, who is always in a good mood, and if she is for once a bit late arriving at an agreed meeting place and we all have to hurry after her, manages to sort everything out without anyone getting the slightest bit tetchy.'

Was it really always like that with Ursula? A unanimous 'yes'. After the opera at Covent Garden they sit together for ages in the craziest (in the most positive meaning of the word) of London restaurants, and exchange views about their recent experience. Ursula's Swiss friends praise *The Magic Flute* to high heaven, with the magnificent Diana Damrau as the Queen of the Night, and start making comparisons with their previous experiences, at the same time discovering great artistic differences in favour of the Royal Opera House. Without going on about her own experiences, or playing the unerring expert, Ursula succeeds in bringing them down to earth from the flies of Covent Garden and pointing out that the opera and ballet of the Lucerne Theatre could be compared favourably with those of the Royal Opera House.

'So why did you lead us then into that temple and let us experience what magnificence can be achieved on a large stage?'

Ursula laughs. The owner of the restaurant, which, in keeping with its environment, bears the name of Sarastro, comes to their table, asks if everything about the food and drinks was all right. He puts his arm around Ursula's shoulder, pulls the charming woman close like a best friend and, with his stunningly roguish smile, asks who these extraordinarily attractive ladies are, whom she has brought to his restaurant at so late an hour. But before Ursula has had time to finish explaining about the commercial school, King Richard, by which name his guests are permitted to call him, calls a waiter over (the best-looking one, please note), and gives him an order in Turkish. Some of Ursula's friends have already been thinking about leaving. King Richard whispers something into Ursula's ear. She is astonished, starts to make a gesture of refusal upon which Richard gently grasps her arm and explains to the company around the table that it would give him the greatest pleasure to invite the pretty girls from the elite Swiss school to fruit, cheese and a glass of champagne. At first hesitantly but then, just as a short while ago in the opera, they applaud. Out of the many loudspeakers placed in the restaurant with all its nooks and crannies, balconies and cosy niches, Diana Damrau is singing Mozart arias. Two waitresses and two waiters are carrying huge dishes overflowing with fruit, and platters with various cheeses to the tables. Another waiter hands a bottle of champagne to Richard. Suitable glasses are set out, the cork pops, the wine foams, the atmosphere is wildly happy. Richard sits down at the table with his special guests and wants to hear what his friend, Madame Ursula, was like as a very young woman. No, not how beautiful she looked, he could see that for himself, and they all had to believe him when he said that among all the illustrious guests who filled his Sarastro evening after evening, before and after the performances in the local theatres, there was no woman more beautiful than Madame Ursula. Applause again, and for *The Magic Flute*, the fruit, the cheese and the champagne.

Ursula used to cycle to the cinema with a friend, from Lucerne to Zurich, where the Albis Pass becomes the Gotthard. There was quite enough music in Lucerne: the best orchestras, soloists and conductors in the world would perform in Lucerne, which was tiny compared to London. Having said that, the concerts were perhaps not for all quite like the Promenade Concerts in the Albert Hall, about which she had raved to everyone. 'One had to be somebody and to be dressed well, black tie, as you say, in order to be let into the old Kunsthaus (House of Art).' And Ursula had known them all personally, had been as close friends with Karajan, Furtwängler, Cantelli, Giulini, Hindemith, Menuhin,

Schwarzkopf and whoever else, as with her former school friends, and many others. But for films, especially the really great French ones, she went by bicycle to Zurich, where her aunt now lived; then, early in the morning, back again to Lucerne. Punctually for the start of school.

'No outrageous exaggerations, please. For one thing, the Albis can't be compared with the Gotthard Pass,' says Ursula dismissively.

King Richard, a Turkish Cypriot, an Ottoman and Oriental, loves stories that do not have to be true, but they do have to sound convincing. After the diploma at the Commercial School for Girls of the City of Lucerne Ursula passed her school-leaving exams at the Kantonschule, the boys' high school in just one year and, after studying in Heidelberg and Geneva, was awarded her translator's diploma with distinction. One of her fellow students in the beautiful Heidelberg —naturally Richard knows all about losing one's heart in Heidelberg— later became a member of the Swiss Federal Council and then President of Switzerland. No, Ursula did not lose her heart to him, socialist though he was.

Richard tells the story of the embassy employee who had to accompany the wife of the Swiss President to the opera, while the big boss was, in the meantime, trying to explain to Downing Street the bank's duty of confidentiality, and some anonymous bank accounts. After the *Entführung aus dem Serail* — 'you know, Mozart had Turkish blood, otherwise he would not have been able to compose that very Turkish story'— the young man ('one of my best friends in diplomacy with a great career ahead of him') arrived with the President's wife for a candle-lit dinner.

Ursula knows that story. She rather doubts whether her former fellow students have been able to follow it, as they might have been confused by the bizarre humour and slight exaggerations of the Sarastro restaurateur. The elderly ladies have nibbled at the seductive fruit, the ripe stilton, cheddar etc., and generously sipped from the champagne glasses. They dismiss her with the words: 'Oh, you can't be more prudish than we were as teenagers.'

Richard asked the President's wife if she was satisfied with the welcome, the service, the drinks, the food, the music from the loudspeakers, and the ambience of his restaurant. 'Thank you, Maestro. More than that.' Pleasantly the compliments went to and fro for a while, as did the smiles. They were getting on well; the embassy employee felt relieved: Sarastro was not always to the taste of guests from Switzerland. Richard asked what it was like to be married to a man who let his wife go to the opera with a subordinate employee while he dined with the prime minister or the Queen. The President's wife liked the charming, if rather direct and casual but very kindly manner of the owner of this restaurant, which would take some beating with its furnishings of gold, and heavy drapes bordering on kitsch. One was accustomed to one's husband's absences necessary for his career and, as he could see, it meant that one had one's own exciting programme. King Richard got her meaning and slid a little closer. He lived around the corner, over there in the Crown Court, a penthouse with an authentic marble Turkish bath. Richard maintains that his invitation, naturally made without any ulterior motive, was taken up by the President's wife. Of course it was not true, but it fitted the style of his fanciful, rambling tales nicely. Apparently the embassy employee was so shocked that he slipped through a crack in the 'Royal Box' of Sarastro, after having mentally drafted his letter of resignation.

Thanks to her good contacts with the embassy, some of this Ursula knows to be more or less true, at any rate the letter of the President's wife: she thanked her diplomatic companion for the extraordinary evening; it had been quite a while since she had been invited by a man beyond all suspicion to a penthouse with a Turkish bath. A fitting letter with which to conclude Ursula's fairy-tale hour from King Richard's 'A Thousand and One Nights'.

The fact that Ursula never spends money on taxis has done the rounds. That she really does give the saved money to support a young brass player, is doubted by some. Not by Richard. He, a Mediterranean opera-lover without equal; he, who will not turn down his music system, even if guests who want to converse, explain to him that they cannot hear themselves speak, makes it equally clear to these guests that he enjoys eating and drinking with great music: without talking over it. Ordinary human voices disturbed those of the works of Mozart, Donizetti, Puccini and Verdi. Even if Wagner did them the honour, there should be no talking; or at least it should be in German, which his friend Ursula spoke perfectly; but she preferred to lose herself in *Tristan und Isolde*, than to natter away parrot fashion, with no one understanding anyway.

Ursula enjoys being driven home by Richard's drivers in the midnight-blue Rolls-Royce Phantom Six. He is an enthusiastic lover of old, exclusive automobiles. Fixed to the front mudguards of his Phantom Six are pennants not belonging to any state or royalty. In London, when Richard's favourite guests are driven home late at night through the hordes of theatre-goers, most of the uninvited spectators might assume that the magnificent vehicle is on its way to Buckingham Palace or some other royal residence. When Ursula sits in the back, alone, perhaps with a last glass of champagne in her hand, her imagination also runs riot with inveterate anti-monarchists. An acquaintance doubting Ursula's charitable inclinations once asked the quite inappropriate question: whether she would then put a tidy sum into her piggy bank marked 'Young Brass' if she had been driven to the grand Hamilton Terrace like the Queen of Sheba in King Solomon's carriage. Ursula replied: 'Especially then. And I double the normal fare.'

During her student days in Heidelberg and Geneva she often hitchhiked, which was quite normal in those days. Not alone, no: she was not that imprudent. But she never, or hardly ever, assumed that there could be men who, in one way or another, were intent on exploiting her carefree nature as if she had no concerns. She could not imagine such people, nor wanted to. At any rate, gullibility was the wrong attribute for a woman who all her life assumed that one should basically trust people: at any rate not mistrust them right from the start. Perhaps from time to time she dismissed too easily the fact that this attitude could be taken advantage of.

In the world of music, despite the nobility of this art, envy and resentment cannot be ruled out, and in science there is just as much elbowing. Ursula vehemently sticks to her maxim that mastery succeeds as much in the music business as in academic competition, and ultimately separates the wheat from the chaff.

As her very elderly mother's brilliance in dealing with her assets and with the Maria und Walter Strebi-Erni Trust started to lose its lustre, and she was perhaps, because of her age, losing some of her phenomenal instinct for security and clarity of vision, Ursula, who had been disinherited because of her marriage to Philip (at that time not considered to be of an appropriate social standing), found that she was confronted more and more with financial matters. Apart from being more than a little preoccupied with happenings in Lucerne and all the activities in London, Ursula found that people were trying to exploit her mother of more than 100 years and also her, the archaeologist and promoter of musicians, for which work she had been decorated by the Queen. She, who was ever more frequently using public transport and had often enough read and heard about cases of need, at the last possible moment, after irregularities too obvious to ignore, put the emergency brakes on and reorganised the board of trustees, and now relies upon people in Lucerne who do not belong to the miserly set. Gone was the untroubled hitchhiker: no more adventures that seemed to turn out all right but were also always a bit risky.

'My various female companions and I had an unwritten rule that the stopping cars had to pass our scrutiny. We made sure of quick escape routes in case a rickety lorry stopped instead of a stylish limousine, or we did not like the look of a driver.'

Occasionally Ursula allowed herself to be tempted by her parents' connections. Why should she forego advantages when her father and mother where acquainted or friends with half the world of those successful, beautiful and rich people? Why not make use of the chance of a room in the Grand Hotel in Florence, made affordable by knowing the owner of the Hotel Wilden Mann in Lucerne? And why not stay in the hotel in Rome where Wilhelm Furtwängler, a close friend of her parents, also stayed? And now, having got her translation diploma, no one could threaten to send her to a reformatory anymore, and no mother in the world could force her to sew her initials onto her clothes, to rubber-stamp her with 'US' as a nobody. Without thinking too highly herself, by the age of only 22 she had mastered four languages and was ready to conquer the world. She only had doubts about her English: she felt she still needed to work at it, and she remembered how, holding Aunt Griti's hand, she had winked at the English tourists on the Schweizerhofquai and had run away if a lord, gentleman or lady spoke to her. So, to England she had to go.

# Chapter 4

## *Switching the Points in Arth-Goldau*

On 8 August 1954 the Philharmonia Orchestra, conducted by Herbert von Karajan, gave its first performance at the International Music Festival in Lucerne. The concert of works by Brahms, Mozart and Ravel, was an outstanding success, not least for Walter Legge, who had founded his Philharmonia Orchestra in 1945. Legge was an English record producer, an extraordinary connoisseur of classical music and a radical perfectionist. Occasionally dissatisfied with the achievements of the orchestras booked for his recordings, he realised his dream of having his own orchestra, which he could train for his recordings and from which he could draw the sound he demanded. That Herbert von Karajan and Wilhelm Furtwängler were rapidly denazified after the war was thanks to Walter Legge. Among others he promoted the soprano Elisabeth Schwarzkopf, and married her.

It was through the International Music Festival in Lucerne that Ursula's father had not only a business relationship but also a friendship with Walter Legge. What a miracle that Ursula's wish to stand on her own two feet in England, no longer dependent on the parents who had for years controlled her upbringing, was to be fulfilled: Walter Legge offered her a job working in the office of the Philharmonia Orchestra. Only six months later she would be orchestral secretary.

Although her affinity for the English had been rather dampened during a short stay near Leeds in the Easter holidays, she packed her bags for the Philharmonia Orchestra and was ready to begin her English adventure and independence. No more 'ifs' or 'buts', even though she had not been particularly thrilled, as a part-time au pair, at having regularly to wash the long-legged underpants of her incredibly tall, stork-like landlord. Her aversion to the unsightly garment stayed with Ursula all her life. In her opinion, even if on top he was dressed in exclusive English cloth, long johns made any man into the kind at whom, even as a child, she would not have winked on the Schweizerhofquai in Lucerne. However frequently their long johns might have been washed, such men were like the Wilhelm Busch characters, into whose bed Max and Moritz were able to place ladybirds with impunity.

The Philharmonia Orchestra, on a tour of Europe, is travelling from Zurich to Milan. Ursula takes the train from Lucerne to Arth-Goldau at the far side of Mount Rigi, changes platforms, the train to Milan arrives, she finds the musicians on it, introduces herself, subjects herself to their scrutiny, only to find that hardly anyone knows who this young woman is or what she has to do with them. A protégée of the Big Boss, it seems.

Ursula is familiar with this sort of thing. In her parents' house, not open to absolutely anybody, she was vividly aware of how important it was to know, at the right time, the right and important people, in order to be accepted into the circle of those who knew where to place the crucial signposts on the routes to success, how to straighten out detours, to eliminate obstacles, to draw road maps showing the way to even more influential people.

Along Lake Uri, the southern section of Lake Lucerne, Ursula says farewell to the peaceful landscape, which she has so often admired from her grandfather's paddle steamer while humming Rossini's tune of Schiller's text from *Wilhelm Tell* to the rhythm of the engine: the up and down of the golden connecting rods and crankshafts. She waits for the church in Wassen, sees the moment coming to show a phenomenon to her fellow-travellers, who surely do not know the area, and explain that it is unique to the entire European rail network.

'Now! Attention please. Up there on the right hand side you will notice a little church, which we will see three times at three different levels. First high up there, hundreds of metres above the track, then level with us, and the third time we will be looking down on the little church of Wassen from much higher up.'

Today she thinks that her enthusiastic guiding through the loop tunnels at Wassen must have seemed like Emil Steinberger's cabaret number *Regardez là l'église*. Anyhow, her promise that the weather on the south side of the Gotthard would be quite different, already Mediterranean, was fulfilled.

Then lots of things happened in a jumbled rush. Now Ursula can only remember that on the evening of her arrival in Milan she was sitting in a box in La Scala, together with Arturo Toscanini and Sergiu Celibidache: both acquaintances of her parents. The little madam had grown into an attractive young woman, and the good looks of both Sergiu Celibidache and Arturo Toscanini put them into Ursula's category of gifted men. And Herbert von Karajan was conducting! It must have been a great evening: thinking back to it now, a magical experience.

The London adventure: in Arth-Goldau with the points in the right position, through the loop tunnels at Wassen, through the Gotthard Tunnel, down through the Leventina to Milan, and there into the box with the man who, at Giuseppe Verdi's funeral, conducted a huge choir singing 'Va, pensiero, sull' ali dorate'. What could go wrong now! Six months had been planned for learning the English language. That they would turn into more than sixty years could not have been foreseen. But her path was marked out by very influential hands. She was thrown straight into the centre of music, into a world in which she had grown up, at any rate at its edges. But now she would be perceived differently from when she had attended receptions at the International Music Festival as a child. Right from the start she no longer wanted to stand, yawning, next to those who patronisingly let the artists understand that, but for them, they would not be able to perform in tails and would only be able to see the nibbles and champagne from a distance. Now she would help organise, make sure that an orchestra was functioning, could go on a stage and be heard.

In the Commercial School for Girls of the City of Lucerne she had learnt the prerequisites for an independent life. And this slogan was true. She could write and speak in the most important languages, could book-keep perfectly, could touch-type, had a reasonably thorough knowledge of the history of her own country and the world, had had the main rules of behaviour conveyed to her, had read not a great but probably a representative amount of literature. As far as travelling was concerned, Ursula had more than an inkling of where her destination would be. To make fun of so-called 'railway geography' is not to Ursula's taste.

As an amusing example of how geography should not be taught, Ursula likes to tell the true story about the daughter of a friend. Class Five of the primary school had to memorise the names on a map of lakes and rivers, mountains and hill ranges, the settlements and railway connections of the department of Entlebuch in the canton of Lucerne, and then be tested on them looking at the same map but without the names. Although the daughter of the friend did not recognise any of the names, she got the highest mark for this test, considered to be extremely difficult. A couple of days later that family travelled in an express train through the said Entlebuch to Bern. At a signal the train made an unscheduled stop at the station in Schüpfheim, one of the names on the map. The eleven-year-old spelled out the name, leant out of the window, saw the station building and the immediate surroundings. Everything looked absolutely real. She rubbed her eyes, sat back in the compartment again and said: 'Schüpfheim. Who would have thought that the place actually exists!'

It was neither quite as bad as that at the Commercial School for Girls nor at the grammar school or the university. But much theoretical information that she could never use later was undoubtedly taught. In languages too. The subjunctive and the past historic. She remembered the French teacher very well, but because of other lessons. Either one had at last mastered the grammar or one more or less left it alone, relied on learning aurally, and best of luck. The teacher spent much more time on old French literature and art history. She could really get her pupils enthusiastic. Rabelais for instance. Ursula starts going into raptures. *Gargantua et Pantagruel*. But Maupassant too: *Le jeu del'amour et du hasard*. Then Camus: *L'Etranger, La Peste*.

Whether she was just as impressed by learning about great literature as by music, which eventually determined her life, she does not know, probably does not want to know. She is a great reader, at any rate.

Another teacher, simply called Miss, fired her enthusiasm for English literature. The words of an anonymous poem accompany her to this day.

'A wise old owl sat in an oak
The more he saw the less he spoke
The less he spoke the more he heard
Why can't we all be like that bird?'

Books, some unfortunately not yet read, are piled up in her office, in the living room, on her bedside table. The CDs are piled even higher. There is a player. But there just is not enough time to hear all these gifts she is constantly getting.

Ursula prefers to hear music live. She wants to experience the people with their instruments. She simply must see music too. Her eyes match her ears. She prefers not to envisage a time when she might not be able to manage the long distances to the many concerts easily anymore, and have to resort, acoustically and optically, to electronic technology: yes, yet more technology.

In England, especially in London, everything was in any case completely different from what she had been accustomed to in her minimally spectacular life up until then: quite an understatement as far as the out-of-the-ordinary was concerned. That is Ursula's way. The out-of-the-ordinary, to her way of thinking, happens somewhere else, not there, where she can bring her influence to bear. That is, if she has ever influenced anything at all. That modesty is a virtue, and only makes sense in the context of Ursula. 'You really did miss something wonderful there', one hears her often maintaining. Long before social media encouraged people to share their experiences, Ursula enjoyed experiencing beauty, excitement, the out-of-the-ordinary together with others: experiencing them live.

Ursula had to cope on her own with getting to grips with her work as orchestral secretary of the Philharmonia Orchestra. For a start she was thrown in at the deep end as far as English currency was concerned, and had to deal with guineas, pounds, shillings and pence. A nightmare. On top of that, none of the musicians were permanently employed. All were freelancers, from the first violin to the man or woman with the triangle. Although the orchestra was made up of regular members, for each engagement the musicians had to be booked individually, chosen according to the programme and repertoire. This was the work of the fixer, with a profound knowledge of the music scene at his or her fingertips. Ursula learnt this job thoroughly and, in the shallow carp pond into which she was thrown for a few pounds a week, had to assert herself against various ravening, profit-seeking pikes. With hindsight it was a hard and, despite some deviousness, best training for her later work as General Manager of the English Chamber Orchestra, co-founded by her. The musicians were paid per concert. The money for the fees always had to be ready. In the middle of the last century the unions had much more power than they generally have nowadays. To pick an argument with them, to go against their written or unwritten rules due to carelessness, was an absolute no-no. There were phases during her time as a fixer when Ursula was looking after several orchestras at once.

It was the great years of the West-End musicals. Everyone was talking about swinging London. The theatres vied with one another with plays that included music, as already started by Gilbert and Sullivan. With singing and dancing, stories of varying quality were told. Rogers and Hammerstein were sure of box-office hits. The demand for actors who could dance, tap-dance and sing was great.

And musicians were needed. For a long time it tended to be male violinists who fixed the orchestras of London's West-End musical scene, and women were also not so often to be found in the cramped orchestra pits. What is known is that Ursula fixed the orchestra for *West Side Story* when it first came to Europe, which caused a bit of a stir as she was neither a violinist, nor male, nor British. Her orchestra was so good that she fixed for several orchestras in the early 1960s, and eventually had five different West End theatre orchestras under her control. The unexpected success of musicals also caused market conditions to change significantly. Musicians who were in tune with the new genres such as Sound and Groove were in demand; they would virtually dance along in the orchestra pit, taking over the tap steps, not just giving the rhythm but becoming part of the collective body.

Whether Ursula sensed her chance to take part in the West End right up at the forefront of things, she cannot recall, but does not completely rule out. In the Drury Lane Theatre at a performance of *My Fair Lady*, in the upper circle, where the acoustics are at their best in most theatres and concert halls, she sits on the edge of her seat, and all the memories of her early time in London come alive again with every song. She shows her infallible instinct for the music in quite another but no less intensive way than when in the Festival Hall she abandons herself completely to the Simon Bolivar Youth Orchestra, Gustavo Dudamel and Olivier Messiaen's *Turangalîla*.

It was a wild epoch, in those hectic times in swinging London, when she was responsible for five West-End orchestras. Next to her normal work she was endlessly searching for musicians who were prepared, next to other more demanding engagements, to play in the theatres on six evenings and at two matinees per week, to increase their earnings with lighter tunes and rhythms.

It was not only with the big orchestras that the unions made sure that their members stuck unconditionally to the rules. Everything was regimented down to the last detail. Without the blessing of the union nothing could be done. It looked after the conditions for its members. The fees were not decided by the musicians but between the orchestras, theatres and unions. If the musicians had been permanently employed, then the unions would undoubtedly have lost their influence.

Every Friday evening Ursula was on the 159 bus on her way to the West End with the fees. She had to deliver the small envelopes punctually. Woe to her if she was late. No fee meant not a note played. For this Ursula was never late. Carefully worked-out routes guaranteed the shortest distances from one theatre to the other. Luckily, she says, the West End does not cover a very large area, the theatres are crowded together in a more or less manageable quarter. Whereas nowadays route, time and place get stored in a computer programme and retrieved at any time, Ursula wrote most of it by hand on appropriately labelled notes. Everything depended upon nothing getting lost en route and the envelopes' contents matching the name of the musician to the last penny; not to mention driving on the left, the notorious London smog and occasional strikes.

She was learning the hard way, pursued by the eagle eyes of previous controllers of the scene; the tiniest mistake, a tear in the net of the lively Swiss woman, would have led to unmitigated disaster. Although Ursula regretted the absence of her parents during the decisive years of her childhood, they had passed on their ever consistent code of morality, which stood her in good stead, if not materially. Morality? A concept that Ursula always approaches with sceptical caution.

When the Tiger Lillies caused a sensation with their bizarre version of the story *Struwwelpeter*, Londoners rushed in hordes to their *Shockheaded Peter*. Ursula neither turned up her nose at nor allowed herself to be influenced by the effusive critics. Thanks to her many connections, she procured tickets absolutely legally for one of the continuously sold-out performances, and allowed herself to be carried away by the euphoric screaming of the predominantly youthful audience and the dyed-in-the-wool Tiger Lillies fans. Rightly, she thought. What was on offer was so expertly original and comical, with the text and music perfectly in tune with the very best West-End productions. Yet Ursula left the theatre deep in thought. *Struwwelpeter* was very much part of her childhood. At that time one had threatened that what happened to the children in the picture book with verses by Dr Hoffmann could just as easily happen to her. The stories that she had just experienced in the perfect show, which had all ended in the death of the 'heroes', were not funny. Ursula had always been curious about anything that she came across. But she never went around with her head in the clouds.

And what about her political correctness? Sometimes Philip Jones was sceptical about it. Once he had finished his career as trumpeter and leader of the Philip Jones Brass Ensemble, he became Head of Wind, Brass and Percussion at the Guildhall School of Music and Drama in the City of London and, some years later, Principal of the renowned Trinity College of Music. The college, the standard of which Philip rapidly restored to that of the best music schools, was then in Mandeville Place in the district of Marylebone. And here, in the very same house, a certain Lilly Langtry had once resided, the mistress of the Prince of Wales, later King Edward VII. Philip's office as Principal of

Trinity College was the famous salon of the lady who had once ruled London's society. At a meeting with Prince Charles the premises in Mandeville Place were mentioned, and Ursula saw the perfect opportunity to ask about the authenticity of the stories that were going around. Prince Charles was amazingly knowledgeable about the affairs of his ancestors, confirmed the temporary residence of the very attractive actress Lilly Langtry, the lover of his great grandfather, and said, before Ursula could ask anything else: 'Yes, she was a remarkable woman.'

Philip, who was familiar with English customs and the behaviour code of subjects towards the royals, stood with knocking knees and face red with embarrassment next to his through-and-through republican wife. It was just like that time, on that rainy coronation day of Elizabeth II, when the outrageous question was asked about the identity of the small man all in white in the open coach next to the oppressively large Queen of Tonga, who was then described as her lunch. As Prince Charles was in a very jovial mood during the conversation in question, Philip feared that Ursula might hit upon the monstrous idea of asking the eldest son of Her Majesty the Queen about his own affairs. He would not have put it past her.

Philip's humour was legendary. If Monty Python had been looking for a crazily funny trumpeter for his *Flying Circus*, the auditions would have got no further than him.

When the Queen Mother awarded Philip the Fellowship of the Royal College of Music, the largely one-sided conversation lasted much longer than normal in such strictly regimented royal ceremonies. Ursula was standing slightly to one side, bursting with curiosity to know what the elderly and much esteemed Queen Mother could possibly have to say of such importance to the man who was repeatedly and humbly nodding his head. When the Queen Mother finally turned to another Fellow, it was not only Ursula who besieged and questioned Philip about the unusually long sermon by the last Empress of India and widow of King George VI. Philip drew Ursula and her curious entourage to one side and repeated at such length what the highly decorated Queen Mother had imparted, that the whole report got very confusing. However, the word-for-word repetition of the royal river of speech was turned into a brilliant cabaret number, which Philip was asked to perform to friends again and again. He would have become rich had he demanded a fee for every performance. It was a hundred-per-cent wordless babbling: a highly intelligent one, Philip never tired of saying. It was Ursula's feeling for political correctness that made her point out to Philip that when making fun of the oldest member of the royal family, once was enough. Philip was shocked but not for long. Then he was astonished and bowed to his wife. Now at last she had become an Englishwoman, he observed proudly and without cynicism.

When the Queen Mother died aged 101 Ursula entered the underground in Warwick Avenue, Little Venice at 10 o'clock in the evening and travelled to Embankment, walked over the Thames via Hungerford Bridge, came across the almost endless procession of mourners, had to go almost as far as Waterloo Station and from there on the far side of the South Bank complex as far as the National Theatre, before she could join the end of the silent and thoughtful queue slowly moving forward along the Thames. After crossing Lambeth Bridge she reached the mediaeval Westminster Hall, was checked by security officials and was able to walk past the coffin, guarded by members of the royal family, and worried about her non-royalist beliefs. After the walk with many strangers who had become friends due to their shared circumstances, she made her way to Trafalgar Square and went by night bus home to St John's Wood. She had gained another experience that she would probably only have once in her life. Morning was approaching. Perhaps it was already dawn as she finished off the long night, not with a strong gin loved by the Queen Mother but with a small glass of Baselbieter Kirsch.

# Chapter 5

## *Signals of Love on a Trumpet*

One day, when Ursula had settled in well behind the scenes of the
Philharmonia Orchestra, extra trumpeters were needed for a
performance of Verdi's *Requiem*. In London, instrumentalists of
all categories were trained in many, perhaps too many schools of
every standard. They all busied themselves in the music market,
they were all more or less ready to be called up, were waiting for
the fixers to remember them and help them get an income, more
often a spare than a fair one. On the lists that Ursula had and to
which she had always systematically added right from the start,
there was also a certain Philip Jones. Twenty-six years old,
trained at the Royal College of Music; from 1948 until 1951
trumpeter in the orchestra of the Royal Opera House, Covent
Garden; founder of the Philip Jones Brass Ensemble and since
1953 trumpeter in the London Philharmonic Orchestra (LPO).
Ursula grabbed the phone, reached the young man, clearly an
ambitious musician who had got it into his head to open for brass
players all doors to serious classical music, until then closed or at
most open just a crack. Like most people, Ursula associated the
signal-blaring trumpet chiefly with military marches, as in
Verdi's triumphal march in his opera *Aida*.

Mr Jones had a particularly pleasant voice, was also extremely
friendly, and listened to the urgent request of the lady from the
Philharmonia Orchestra with an appealing accent and perfect
English. 'Very tempting. Great piece of music.' But unfortunately
there was a cricket match with the LPO team booked on that day.
No, impossible to postpone this event. His colleagues would
never forgive him if he chose Verdi over an assignment in white
flannel trousers, a white shirt and sleeveless pullover.

Well yes, the man tried his hardest to make his refusal
comprehensible. But what on earth was cricket? What was more

important to a trumpeter, in an admittedly renowned orchestra, than to perform Verdi's *Requiem* with the Philharmonia Orchestra? Wasn't cricket that game on a groomed lawn where, with a long-handled wooden hammer, you had to hit a ball, also of wood, through variously coloured wire hoops, meanwhile drinking tea, eating sandwiches, cultivating high-flown conversation, not to mention drinking whisky with very British affectation.

Ursula found her twelfth trumpeter, Verdi's *Requiem* went well, and she could not get Philip Jones, born in 1928 in Bath to a family of brass players, out of her head, although probably unconsciously. What if he was the kind of Englishman she had secretly admired as a child on the promenade of the Schweizerhofquai in Lucerne?

Later, not very much later, but definitely without any ulterior motive, she was able to engage Philip Jones for another concert. There was no alternative. His curriculum vitae was in order, and what he intended with his brass ensemble, which he had founded a couple of years before, might turn out to be quite exotic. With other enthusiastic brass players he had managed to free the trumpet from the war-like blasting in four-four time, and made it so that it no longer had to be played in marching uniforms. That would be a bonus towards which Ursula might even be able to contribute, as well as engaging the self-conscious trumpeter.

He was handsome. Furthermore, his appearance, always in modest yet all the more cultured attire, absolutely matched Ursula's picture of Englishness. It was easy to complete and enhance her picture of the flamboyant pre-war British tourists with this cultured young man. He had quite a different sense of humour from those of her fleeting acquaintances in Lucerne, Heidelberg or Geneva, with their rather coarse jokes.

Ursula was not blinded by love, even though in retrospect it might have seemed like the obvious cliché. On the contrary, she kept her eyes wide open and prepared her senses for all the wonderful signals that Philip tried to send her with his trumpet.

'After Philip turned down the first engagement I approached him with, I accepted his first proposal to engage me for life, without cricket, crocket or whatever other possible hindrances, without any ifs or buts.'

It did not occur to Ursula to consider family bonds or restricting conventions. The English, after all, were guaranteed to belong to the most important tourists of the top drawer, approved of even by Ursula's parents. And, already after a short while as an orchestral secretary, she was more than just vaguely aware that London was a city of music in which concerts were performed at festival standard all the year round. Handel's *Water Music* flowed down the Thames long before Strauss's *Blue Danube* babbled along to Vienna, and Elgar's *Pomp and Circumstance, March No.1* would always be a match for the *Radetzky March*.

Philip Jones's explanation as to why he had founded his own ensemble and had wanted to make a lasting mark, made the same sense as Ursula's wish to be together with a man who challenged her curiosity, was prepared to share her unbridled vitality, who would never ask her, as a neighbour did years later: 'For God's sake, Mrs Jones, when are you going to change your impossible way of life?'

For three years Philip Jones sat as a promising trumpeter in the orchestra pit of the Royal Opera House, Covent Garden, his trumpet on his lap, and counted the endless bars in which he had nothing to do before his next entry. It bored him silly to be sitting down there on the backbenches, like an insignificant Member of Parliament in the House of Commons. Yet this son of a musical family, his father a trombonist, his uncle a trumpeter, had studied barely four years, with the best, most renowned professors of brass, yet achieved the highest grades. Even with the best intentions, the creators of the most popular operas did not give a trumpet as many entries as the strings.

His first ensemble was primarily for renaissance and baroque music, and was limited to two trumpets and two trombones. But Philip did not want to concentrate exclusively on ancient music and then perhaps get stuck with it. He expanded the ensemble for later music, turning it from a quartet into a quintet for two trumpets, trombone, horn and tuba. It needed perseverance, not just on the part of the instrumentalists. The ways of the music scene could not so easily be changed: although the quartet and quintet met with much goodwill, the loud, blasting instruments could not fill even small concert halls with audiences, let alone larger ones, which should have brought in the necessary money.

Philip's fellow players were all members of the best London orchestras. Perseverance became long lasting perseverance. Ten years after the founding of the Philip Jones Brass Ensemble, the latter, with its leader, became the illustrious quintet with the trumpeter, arranger and conductor Elgar Howarth, the horn player Ifor James, the trombonist John Iveson and the unique tuba player John Fletcher. Those most reputable names from the guild of brass players drew attention to the ensemble and its innovative musical arrangements, and suddenly there were sounds that made people prick up their ears. Here were five soloists who together played works previously not heard by an ensemble exclusively of brass players. The critics of serious newspapers and magazines, as well as radio stations, wrote and spoke of a brass revolution. Yet the breakthrough bided its time.

In England as well as in Switzerland, brass bands played at a sometimes astoundingly high standard. In the industrial north of England there were many brass bands with union connections. There were regional and national competitions. The multiple award-winning film *Brassed Off* produced by Mark Herman is a magnificent but also tragic testament to English brass music. Here too the great, popular hits are played. *Land of Hope and* Glory from Elgar's *Pomp and Circumstance, March No.1* is celebrated, just as on the last night of the Proms, the traditional series of summer concerts in the Royal Albert Hall. The film dates from the year 1996 and covers the coalminers' crisis at the time of the Iron Lady, Mrs Thatcher.

Philip Jones's commitment to cultivating a new image for brass playing had begun thirty years earlier. In *Brassed Off*, works by Gioachino Rossini and Joaquín Rodrigo are played. There was not one of the musicians playing in the film band who had not heard of Philip Jones. It is no different nowadays: one just has to ask a trumpeter, a horn player, a trombonist or tuba player, in an orchestra anywhere in the world, if the name Philip Jones means anything to them. A light in the eyes of those questioned tells all.

Ursula's husband remains the indisputably great revivalist of brass chamber music.

The actual breakthrough dates back to the beginning of the 1970s and also, unsurprisingly, to Ursula Jones. She, who is still responsible for a lively exchange of young, talented musicians between Switzerland and Great Britain and is tirelessly on the look out for top talents, secured the engagement of the Philip Jones Brass Ensemble (PJBE) by the International Music Festival in Lucerne. Ursula was mainly wishing to make a tour of Switzerland possible. However, the concert organisers did not trust the quintet to attract enough audiences, so for the Migros-Klubhaus concerts three extra trumpets and trombones were added. The formation with four trumpets, four trombones, horn and tuba managed to fascinate the audiences just as the English tourists on the Schweizerhofquai had once fascinated little Ursula. Whether the one experience left an impression as long as the other, remains an open question. What was certain was that the appealing and showy brass players had more to offer than those Britons who regarded their luxury hotels as their last remaining colonies.

Without ingratiating himself with the audience, Philip Jones knew how to win not only their ears but their hearts with folksong arrangements. If Philip and his fellow musicians, with the by now very typical PJBE sound, started up their encore 'Vo Luzän gäge Wäggis zue' and set a rhythm that got everyone swaying happily, it was for Ursula like being back on her grandfather's paddle steamer. The controller of the engines, the gleaming connecting rods and drive shafts, the man who looked like Bernard Shaw, the conjuror with the doll's houses and mechanical toys, would have been proud of his favourite granddaughter's husband.

Back again 'on the island', Philip Jones remained faithful to his successfully newly created formation. It became the 'Swiss formation' with four trumpets, a horn, four trombones and a tuba. Since then this group of ten is known worldwide as a Philip Jones formation and can, where necessary, be added to, expanded and reorganised according to the musical work. A certain amount of murmuring went around the institutions of serious music when Philip, together with Elgar Howarth, arranged Mussorgsky's

*Pictures at an Exhibition* for brass instruments. The enlarged brass ensemble plus two percussionists created a sensation. The critics poured eulogy upon eulogy onto the PJBE. The brass had discarded the marches, but not entirely.

With a yet more enlarged group, the Philip Jones Wind Ensemble, a veritable wind orchestra, Philip had the idea of making gramophone recordings of the best known marches by the American composer John Philip Sousa. These incomparable evergreens became a bestseller. Even today the marches bring in quite a lot of royalties. In accordance with Philip Jones's will, and with Ursula's permission, the money goes entirely to the Royal Society of Musicians (RSM), founded in 1738 by G.F. Handel. For many years Philip was a member of this charitable organisation, whose aim is to support older musicians and those who have hit on hard times.

The more famous the PJBE became, the more music had to be arranged. Apart from the works by Giovanni Gabrieli and Johann Pezelius there was hardly any music purely for brass. For critical audiences Philip and his brass players were ever more frequently needed for performances of choral works, especially those by Monteverdi. They enjoyed a very fruitful collaboration with the London Bach Choir for many years.

What Ursula had suspected and, with her acute sense for the exceptional, had foreseen, came to pass: the PJBE turned into a success story. There was worldwide applause, honours followed innumerable awards and prizes. If only there had not been that matter of the love affair with Ursula Strebi, the young Swiss woman from a somewhat better family, rooted in classical music.

Ursula Strebi was happily in love and on the way to not quite conquering the world but at least finding out about it; a world, which in London seemed to her, in the centre of what was once an empire, to be somewhat greater, more open and tolerant than the town with its court church, its Kunsthaus, Chapel Bridge and Jesuit church. This world let her parents know, as was fitting, that she had fallen in love with an Englishman, or more precisely, a Welshman. He was also a musician, which must please her father, the co-founder of the International Music Festival in Lucerne, and her mother, hostess of innumerable parties full of festival guests.

The orchestra of the Royal Opera House, Covent Garden, and the London Philharmonic Orchestra, were institutions that had a place in the sacred halls of music, which the International Music Festival still had to attain. Ursula, who engaged musicians daily and knew exactly how much was in the payday envelopes, and had to be careful not to pick a fight with the unions, by now knew what she was about, knew what Philip Jones was worth in the music market.

In leisurely Lucerne her parents had no idea about any of this. In actual fact it was only in the summer that there was ever anything much going on in Lucerne, whereas in London it was festival time all year round, and in the Promenade Concerts in the Royal Albert Hall first-class music was played, and not only to the sort of people who could afford the more expensive seats or suitable attire for entry into the Kunsthaus. Once the musical world realised what Philip Jones intended to do with his brass ensemble, it was this very world that he would change.

Her parents were horrified. The basis of a marriage could not be the kind of music that was not to be heard in temples such as the Lucerne Kunsthaus.

'Never. Forget it! Forget him!'

'Never. He's the one. Forget me as I was in Lucerne!'

Ursula was no longer a child whom one could threaten with an approved school, or could order to sew initials onto her clothes; moreover her father and mother were far too busy even remotely to carry through the ban that seemed more like an ultimatum. A year was needed to think it over. If the love lasted a year, then the tiresome affair could be brought up again. From now on no more contact. In Lucerne 'out of sight, out of mind' is still true. As far as Walter and Maria Strebi-Erni were concerned the Philip Jones chapter was, for the time being, closed. Another, better partner would turn up for Ursula. One was, after all, someone; one had been a city councillor and, after the war, had made one's name as a lawyer. If one invited people to parties, the guests came, and ever more frequently illustrious ones. It would be laughable if, in the social sphere of the better circles, a Mr Right failed to cast an eye on the pretty, world-savvy daughter. One just had to keep an eye open and to take appropriate precautionary measures; if necessary to arrange a return journey from sinful London. It was not that one was friendly with the owner of the Philharmonia Orchestra to no avail. Walter Legge would surely put things right.

Ursula stayed where she was. London was a Moloch of a city. The detailed supervision of the agreed distance between the secretary of the Philharmonia Orchestra and the trumpeter of the London Philharmonic Orchestra was not possible. That an unknown trumpeter, as Ursula's parents disrespectfully dismissed him, would become an icon, decorated by the Queen with high honours, was not written in the stars over Lucerne; at any rate the clear enough signs were not recognised. But what was known to those in Lucerne was that there were socially, financially secured and smoothly functioning networks that had to be maintained with the skill and care of the old school.

The daughter, however, spread quite a different net underneath her unbroken relationship and built up a secret service that functioned so sensitively that the tiniest tremor was detected and a warning signal sent. If necessary, this would initiate a mighty furore among the trumpets, trombones, horns and tubas of all the London orchestras, and make the strings of every violin, viola, cello and double bass vibrate. But this was beyond the imagination of her clueless parents who, as a precaution, had already laid on the table the threat of disinheriting their daughter.

# Chapter 6

## *'Ursi', the Secret Service*

Ursula at no time considered distancing herself from Philip Jones. On the contrary. Naturally she kept her home and address in London, but soon moved in with Philip. A bad conscience? Absolutely not. Why should her parents, who had never really taken care of her, suddenly start playing the concerned mother hen? Father and Mother need not know about her breaking her agreement to maintain radio silence for a year. London was not Lucerne, where literally everyone knew everyone else, where a rumour did not even need to be let loose in the town in order for it to become one. 'Did you know?' 'Have you already heard?' It would have caused irreparable damage if people had passed it around, at first behind their hands, and soon after quite openly, that the daughter of the respected couple was living in so-called sin in London. Yet Ursula's parents were not even Catholic.

In London Ursula was able to cross the Thames on the Tower, Blackfriars, Waterloo, Hungerford, Westminster, Lambeth, Vauxhall, Albert, Battersea, Wandsworth, Putney and Hammersmith bridges, without being recognised by anybody among the crowds of passers-by. In Lucerne, as the daughter of her parents, she would not have been able to take one step over the Seebrücke, the Kapellbrücke, the Ratshausbrücke, the Reusssteg or the Spreuerbrücke without being recognised, addressed, jealously stared at, ignored, or given a disapproving look. The English were actually notorious for barely looking people in the eye, on public transport, on all those full-up buses and underground trains, for avoiding any visual contact, for not complimenting a woman with a shy smile.

Nevertheless, caution was advisable. Telephoning was, in the 1950s, an extremely expensive business, and well off people were always more thrifty than lackadaisical have-nots. In order to receive a telegram one had to be at home, and Ursula had to be contactable by her parents. But to be contactable in the years 1954-5 was quite a different matter from what it is nowadays. Letters from abroad took a few days. Yet it was very useful for a young, unmarried woman during an extended absence always to have a watertight alibi to hand.

'Jessie's Friends' were Ursula's security service, thus 'Ursi' (as in 'Stasi'). No one was spied on, listened into, under surveillance or, by means of perfidious machinations, declared an enemy. It was only about security from her parents, and involved relatives, friends and acquaintances of the 'young and beautiful Swiss girl with her gorgeous trumpeter'.

Until now, more than sixty years later, those of 'Jessie's Friends' still living meet at least once a year for a celebratory meal with hundreds of stories to tell. And at these merry get-togethers, never are the same events, doings, virtual abductions, aggressive letters, tomfooleries or emergencies talked about. Sometimes details of the reminiscences might get a bit mixed up, this and that are forgotten, so that two supposedly separate stories might sound almost the same. The ageing secret agents of the past were agreed that the potential for boredom diminished with age. Due to their reduced powers of recollection, many of the old repeated stories seemed as though they were being told for the first time: how Ursula and Philip could realise their love, thanks to the cheerful, selfless efforts of 'Ursi', completely undisturbed by the sword of Damocles forged in Switzerland.

Officially Ursula was living with Jessie Hinchliffe, one of the first violins in the Philharmonia Orchestra. Ursula's eyes start to shine when she speaks of Jessie.

In Ursula's life there is no downtime: every day comes up with new, unexpected occurrences to which she naturally applies herself, and her memory store in her restless (in the most positive sense of the word) life is inexhaustible, in a chest bolted with a heavy lock; the kind, in the adventure stories of long ago, that was brought to distant islands by more or less Christian seafarers, to be kept safe from pirates. Perhaps the laughing teddy bear also came out of such a treasure chest.

The secret behind Ursula's happy temperament, her positive, cheery attitude to everyday matters really is down to a nondescript toy bear, which, should a shadow happen to fall over her much admired busyness, she takes in both hands, cradles backwards and forwards until, out of its belly, infectious laughter begins and Ursula's slightly jaded mood climbs hand over fist up to a major key. It is as easy as that.

There is no need for a laughing bear when thinking about Jessie Hinchliffe. The attractive woman in the first violins was one: she was the unique woman in Ursula's life. A substitute mother as Aunt Griti once was. At the word substitute Ursula hesitates for a moment. No, she no longer needs to trouble the bear anymore either. You always need a spare if the original no longer works.

In the middle of the mostly highly amusing stories all about the 'Ursi' duties, Ursula is suddenly caught by a silent seriousness. That first meeting with Jessie Hinchliffe must have been quite an occasion. At first glance there was a mutual liking. On the one hand the young woman, completely inexperienced in love and many other feelings, yet highly efficient as an orchestral secretary; on the other hand the violinist with an experience of life which enveloped her as in an aura, and had an effect on Ursula's curiosity, on her interpersonal shortcomings, like a magic spell. It would never have occurred to Jessie to force herself onto Ursula, and Ursula would never have dared to get close to the woman whom she engaged for orchestras. It just happened; without doing anything or causing a stir. No blushing. No barriers between the 'little Swiss girl' and perhaps the rather high-spirited lady in the first desk of the violins. And the male musicians, who, without dominating, were in the majority, did not only play along but were enjoying the sheer pleasure of belonging to 'Ursi'. Of course, no one worked under the code word 'Ursi'. Next to Jessie and her friend Molly Barger, the violinist Hans Geiger also belonged, and his Swiss wife Hanni, the cellist Dorothy and her husband, Béla Dekany, leader of the BBC Symphony Orchestra, as well as the harpist Sidonie Goossens, who came from a legendary musical family.

After concerts Jessie often invited people to women-only parties. A sensation. Not only for Ursula. Even in the liberal and already swinging London the gentlemen, who were used to men-only evenings and clubs, looked on suspiciously, turned up their noses and, as well as a resurrection of the suffragettes, suspected such erotic deviations as those which, decades before, had landed Oscar Wilde in prison. All day and in the evenings they were embedded in orchestras predominantly of men, and following an even more dominating conductor, were playing beautifully, and afterwards indulging in malicious talk in private flats, in salons and the backrooms of dimly lit pubs, as if they were men. Nothing but jealousy and silly chat. Ursula goes into raptures about those women-only gatherings, which opened her eyes to a life without sanctimonious and high-flown morals. What her mother had caused, with all her failings and threats, sending her daughter completely unprepared and naïve into life, Jessie Hinchliffe explained to Ursula quite naturally and, more importantly, with endless fun.

Every now and then Ursula's mother announced that she was visiting London. The city attracted her too, aroused her curiosity. She too wanted to recover, in a somewhat larger world, from the strolls on the never-changing Schweizerhofquai, from those really rather short bridges, the theatre on the River Reuss, and the Kunsthaus, open to everyday visitors outside the weeks of the festival. In this city her mother had lost some of her self-assurance when, with a mischievous friendliness, Ursula introduced her to her friends. And 'Ursi' held fast. The daughter was portrayed and praised as a paragon of virtue. Ursula offered her services as a guide to traditional London, doing one or two diversions to places she had recently got to know. After a short time the world of music had unreservedly opened to her and, with her natural, and no less winning charm, she was gladly received even when she was not doing the rounds with the fees envelopes.

Jessie, Molly, Hans, Hanni, Dorothy, Béla and Sidonie made sure that Philip Jones did not by chance come across the attractive mother and her cheerful daughter. 'Ursi' without a doubt crossed one or two boundaries, cheated here and there, led the woman to believe certain things, the woman who had thrown a spanner in the works of the union between the gifted and also superbly good-looking trumpeter and the equally gifted Philharmonia secretary. Ursula was even threatened with the withdrawal of parental love and the carefully calculated and considerable inheritance, if the heart were to overrule reason.

Ursula had justified doubts about the cloak of perfection that 'Ursi' had thrown over her. Did the mother, who had seen enough to make her think of her child as a 'wicked' girl, believe all these compliments about her well brought up daughter?

The London programme, which they had thought out with Ursula for Mrs Strebi, did not leave much time for anyone to wonder whether such an urbane daughter was perhaps not on the lookout for a future husband at all. Perhaps they had discovered Ursula's phenomenal talent with which, even now, she leads culturally interested tourist groups from a museum to a concert, to another museum with the most sensational exhibitions, from there to the opera or a theatre, then to the most spectacular hidden gastronomical delights, and to her distinguished friends. It requires robust health and a great multicultural interest to be led by Ursula through London, to go with her to Glyndebourne, Garsington, Bath, Cornwall, Oxford, Cambridge and other highlights. And one should pay attention to what she says. Always having to repeat things or correct anything wrongly pronounced takes up too much time, so that there is not enough for something else that must not be missed, or to make a diversion to something out of the ordinary, or even to discover something new oneself.

After a late evening meal in the club of the Royal Overseas League or in the intimate atmosphere of Ursula's club, The Two Brydges, the privileged friends, having had every last drop of attentiveness squeezed out of them, fall exhausted into bed, just as, over sixty years ago, her mother did on her trip to check up on the abstinence of her daughter. No more questions. The next day would be even fuller, and everything Ursula imparted about all that was worth seeing, hearing and experiencing would by far exceed the capacity of any normal powers of absorption.

Ursula's mother, née Maria Erni, was an extraordinarily strong, exceedingly self-willed personality, whom no one in social, or particularly in financial matters, could begin to match. Years later, after her husband's death in 1981, she bought the beautiful house at the top of the Lucerne Rebstockhalde for Ursula and Philip. 'So that you have something in Switzerland.' True to character, however, she remained the owner and determined who was permitted to enjoy the unique view onto Lake Lucerne. She also made sure that none of her assets would ever disappear in the direction of England.

Were the conditions attached to the house perhaps a delayed revenge for the tricks of the 'Ursi'? They had made as if her daughter was adhering strictly to her agreement to put her love for the English 'nobody' on ice for a year, to see if it was worth tying herself to him forever. But the love was too hot, even if a delayed spring had tried to make a difference: the freezing point could not be reached, either in Celsius or Fahrenheit.

The couple were in slight danger of the owner of the Philharmonia Orchestra, Walter Legge. For no obvious reason the influential music producer had strange reservations about the universally popular and valued trumpeter and committed revivalist of brass music. Legge was married to the soprano Elisabeth Schwarzkopf. Both were friends of Walter and Maria Strebi.

Walter Legge was the director of EMI and producer of many innovative records of great works, and undoubtedly too much of a gentleman to advise his clever orchestral secretary, Ursula Strebi, against the trumpeter, Philip Jones. He also had too professional an instinct for the exceptional, for him not to have noticed Philip. But he had probably been secretly made aware by Ursula's father of the unpopular liaison between a brass player and the inexperienced and unenlightened daughter. After all, one knew from first-hand experience how the gentlemen in the back rows of the orchestra, when their lips were not pressed against their mouthpieces, were prone to show the frivolous side of music making.

But Philip did not belong to those who, for instance at Glyndebourne, used the intervals to drive to a pub a bit further afield in order to drink a few of pints of beer and then were back again in the orchestra pit with a full bladder to play, somewhat more restrainedly, their part in Wagner's *Tristan und Isolde*. It did not even always have to be Wagner for one to be noticeable in the orchestra and to blast oneself onto the conductor's memory. Philip was in the most positive sense an uninhibited trumpeter. Otherwise he would never have managed to tear those brightly gleaming instruments out of their deep orchestral sleep, to take them out of their military and signalling mode, and to prove that chamber music could be played and interpreted with trumpets, horn, trombones and tuba, just as it had been reserved for strings, woodwind, occasionally harp and predominantly the piano. As a person, Philip knew to act with exemplary moderation. With his wide-ranging humour he needed no alcoholic stimulation.

With his beautiful, slightly ageing Porsche, which knew the garage in the mews like a well-studied score, he turned out into Hamilton Close and noticed that his instrument in its case was not on the passenger seat. Philip drove back and the case he had left in the garage just missed going under a back wheel, where it had actually gone a short while before in a hotel garage in France: a further sign that it was time to lay the instrument to rest where Providence had intended its destruction. Instead of being in charge of the PJBE he offered his services to the Musicians Benevolent Fund (now Help Musicians UK), and later became Principal of Trinity College of Music.

He was already a member of the Worshipful Company of Musicians and was driving back home from a black-tie dinner with a friend. At Smithfield he turned off, wanting to show his friend the church in which he and Ursula were married, and hit upon a police control. Philip was and remained convinced that they tended to go for toffs in swish cars, and enjoyed the satisfaction of catching the chaps who, in their stiff shirts and collars, thought they were allowed to drive while drunk. The test showed an alcohol level minimally over the limit, the driving licence was confiscated, and Philip phoned Ursula from the police station to ask her to fetch him and drive them home in the undamaged Porsche. For two years he was not allowed behind the wheel. For two years he went on foot along the Regent's Canal as far as the zoo and from there to his office in Mandeville Place. He had just become Principal of Trinity College of Music, and he and

Ursula were able to keep secret the facts about driving in a 'drunken' state. It could have cost him his reputable position, just when he had been invited to take it on with a view to polishing up the somewhat blemished image of the college, rather like that of a trumpet tarnished by verdigris.

When absolutely necessary Ursula acted as his chauffeuse. Nobody was bothered that the well-known musician and twice-decorated principal of the college, with its reputation restored, let himself be driven, as more or less befitted his status. On his walks along the secluded canal, past the zoo and through the extensive park, he got to know flora and fauna throughout the seasons better than many a qualified zoologist or botanist. He was on familiar terms with all the herons, whooper swans, monkeys and camels.

Apart from the person with him on the fateful drive, and Ursula, no one ever got to know about the confiscation of the driving licence. Philip felt he had the pursuers of black ties to thank for the fact that the story did not get flushed through dubious channels to the gutter press. Only after his death did Ursula, on carefully selected occasions, allow it to filter gently through why she had become the rather unconventional driver of an honoured man who had been made by the Queen a CBE, Commander of the Order of the British Empire, and become honorary member of many institutions. No one seemed particularly surprised: Philip was just as careful about his reputation as he was about stuffing the sleeves of his jackets with tissue paper after taking them off, and never failing to use wooden shoetrees. But they also knew that he would have laughed with others about his bad luck.

The year of abstinence, or rather the intended seeing through of the year of estrangement ordered by Ursula's parents, led, thanks to 'Ursi' and the enlightened influence of substitute mother Jessie, to a very deep consolidation of the relationship between Ursula and Philip. The two lived on a lonely island, dreamed of by so many of the young in love, with many well-meaning natives concerned in securing aphrodisiacs soaked in milk and honey, keeping any disturbing elements away, and building a protective wall by not always quite legal and thus all the more colourful means.

No wonder that Ursula, without the slightest hesitation, was able to tell her parents that the imposed separation had had the effect that, for a whole year, she had thought of nothing except Philip, and neither had he of her; because they had not been able to see or hear one another, everyday life had been a blank.

There had never been any disagreement, they had never been in danger of taking offence at an unexpected, unpleasant character trait. He had not been able to get annoyed by her smoking habit, nor had she been able to dwell on his reservations about certain interpretations of the works of Mahler and Bruckner. Squeaky clean and brand new they would have imagined themselves to be as man and wife, because they had not been allowed to get sight of a single piece of each other's dirty linen.

Her mother did not understand, did not want to understand, that her aversion to Philip was as counterproductive as anything could be; her father never had any doubt about his decree, which, legally speaking, should have led to a verdict. But they had to realise that they had got nowhere with their 'prohibited' notices. Ursula's parents were facing a very human heap of shards, which, for the rest of their lives, they would never be able to dispose of in any befitting manner.

# Chapter 7

## *The Suitcase is with the Sacristan*

'To marry or not to marry, that was never the question.' And 'whether', some reasonably rational couples in Ursula's and Philip's situation should have asked themselves. Stinking rich Walter and Maria Strebi-Erni were not. Not yet. The success of the law practice and the International Music Festival in Lucerne, the absolutely infallible feel that her mother had for money and how it could be, and had to be, invested profitably, guaranteed reliable prognoses. As a musician and music agent Ursula could at one time have slipped into a golden nest and, with the prospect of a certain inheritance, been without any existential anxieties.

So what. Ursula had long since plumbed the depths of her abilities. With her natural charm and her infectious and consistently good humour, she could bring all her kinds of knowledge down to a common denominator, and expand her talents, perhaps inherited from her parents. Then life, without the advantage of powerful connections, could be more satisfactorily mastered on her own, than with the threat of having, over and over again, to sew the hideously decorated initials onto one's clothes.

And Philip would never have to live on the breadline, as so many in the musical world did. As he as well as Ursula was sure, he was predestined to follow a path shining with brass instruments. His brass ensemble would be in everyone's ears and on everyone's lips. So:

'A few more hours, that's all the time I got
A few more hours before I tie the knot
I'm gettin' married in the morning
Ding, dong, the bells are gonna chime
But get me to the church on time'

The tune would have been suitable, the words perhaps less so. The traditional hen night would have been in the 'Ursi' style, and, of all the Queen's subjects in the United Kingdom, there must have been one or two women who would gladly have taken the place of the slender Swiss girl at the altar, alongside the fine figure of Philip Jones. As a musician Philip would hardly have had anything against the earworms of Frederick Loewe, and as Alan J. Lerner had used a text by George Bernard Shaw to go with them, Ursula would have had no objection either. Philip was not an obstinately classical man. He even played with The Beatles. The unusual fascinated him more than the well known, and if he had the chance to support anything ground-breaking, his enthusiasm knew no bounds. When his friend and lifelong companion, Elgar Howarth, was asked if he would collaborate with Frank Zappa in making a record, he asked Philip's opinion. 'Doesn't Frank Zappa need two trumpets?' asked Philip. Frank Zappa would have said yes at once. Unfortunately, Philip was unavailable due to another engagement.

One can easily imagine the ceremony in the Church of St Bartholomew the Great, in Smithfield in the City. Everyone would be there: the complete 'Ursi', a cheerful crowd, and the vicar literally infected by the Groove of Philip's friends. The Wedding March, which he as the bridegroom would probably not play in, would sound like an invitation to dance.

It turned out quite differently. The wedding party was very small and modest. The famous horn-player, Dennis Brain (1921-1957), played the organ, and Philip's Uncle Roy the trumpet.

It would have been interesting to fathom the feelings of the mother. Yes, she had actually come over for the wedding of her only child. Her father had not been able to bring himself to walk up the aisle next to Ursula, feeling in the breast pocket of his dinner jacket the letter in which he explained unequivocally that his daughter would have to do without any inheritance, even the statutory portion. They must have had hearts of stone to make that decision. It must have been a gargantuan achievement for the mother who, in the church and at the wonderful wedding feast with enchanting guests that followed, was obliged to look amiable in the face of the wicked game she had so disapproved of.

Not so with acquiring the wedding rings. Ursula had for ages longed for a Vespa but which was so expensive that for the sealing of their matrimony they would only have been able to put curtain rings on their fingers. They, or rather Philip, then after all decided on a better, in fact a diamond one, and Ursula postponed her wish for the timeless, stylish Italian cult scooter. Forever. So she would not after all dare to be a match for the beautiful Roman women, Gregory Peck and Audrey Hepburn, which one would not have put it past her to be.

After twenty years of marriage Ursula's ring got lost while washing up after a party in their house in Hamilton Terrace. The atmosphere after the guests had departed was not particularly good. Too many empty bottles and glasses, lots of dishes, left-over food, greasy cutlery, red wine and coffee stains on a very old lace cloth, which was not easy to wash, heaps of pans. Philip's willingness to help was for once below the lowest level, and because there was no dishwasher in the kitchen yet, the loss of her wedding ring seemed to Ursula nothing but one more of a whole string of disasters. Forget it! And there was no question of a stroke of fate, a higher force or some such nonsense. Soon after this happening a replacement, which did not reduce the budget unduly, was bought in an absolutely ordinary jewellery shop on Oxford Street. Ursula never agreed with Marilyn Monroe when the Hollywood icon sang 'Diamonds are a girl's best friend.'

Like a good omen for the marriage that defied all upsets on an endless scale, the ring that had been assumed lost turned up again. It had got in between the very old and very fine napkins, reserved for special occasions: family heirlooms with an undoubtedly conspiratorial cast of mind.

It seems that Ursula is inclined occasionally to lose 'very important' things. If the missing valuables do not turn up after a reasonable time, she, for whatever reason, loses all interest in them. As she anyway does not have the time to examine the reasons for her behaviour, even the most valuable objects lose their value.

A few years ago when Ursula came back to London from the Lucerne Festival, she could not find in her small rucksack a leather pouch with old and newer jewellery that she had taken with her from London, in order, if necessary, to wear at receptions that she had to attend in her capacity as a board member of the festival. She had very little luggage as she had kept a supply of clothes in her then family house in the Rebstockhalde. In the rucksack she only had bare necessities and the jewellery, now no longer there. Yes, worth a fortune. For a start the necklace that Paul Sacher had, on her fiftieth birthday, casually hung around her neck. A hundred pearls. Real ones. What else? From the house of Hofmann-Sacher. Telephone calls to Lucerne and searches in various places led nowhere. Ursula would not contemplate theft. Who would have helped themselves to her property? She had lost the jewellery, and it was her fault. Only an idiot would not have kept a bag found without an address with it. Insured? What was the point of spending a lot of money which could be of use elsewhere. A young woman or man studying at a music college could live for half a year or more off the money with which she might have insured things that she hung around her neck, around her wrists or on her ears, never all at the same time and at most once or twice a year. She was not prepared to mourn over genuine pearls and precious stones that she had taken possession of but not purchased herself. On the advice of a friend she looked in an inner compartment of her rucksack, to see if the jewellery had got amongst the bundle of spare underwear, just as the wedding ring had among the napkins after the ignominious argument in the kitchen. Never before had she stormed down the sixty steps from the bedroom to the kitchen so quickly, in order to tell her friend that she had actually found the jewellery, just as she had suspected, among her underwear. Once Ursula had got her breath back, her mood suddenly became serious, almost melancholy. She wondered how she could get rid of the jewellery that she had already written off.

Her will, already written, and agreed with Philip, exclusively to help the promotion of young musicians and the support of older colleagues in difficulties, is a record of her philanthropy.

Another heirloom is a Rolex Oyster. Ursula's father, in a fit of generosity, left it to Philip. One day this jewel of precision had disappeared. The sadness over the loss of the precious watch, as in the case of the wedding ring and jewellery, was limited. Many years later, when Philip had already died, the Korean home help, who once a week, with inimitable exactness, tackled the dust of the city and the overgrown garden, found the watch, which, in her opinion, was very old fashioned. It came to light when, after a burst pipe, she pulled every single book in Philip's large music library off the shelves and, however old they were, restored them to their original shininess, first with a damp, then with a dry cloth. She shook the stopped masterpiece of watchmaking and was amazed when the Oyster immediately started to tick, as if in this almost sacred room, the ever-present Mr Philip had breathed new life into the watch. The former Korean junior champion dropped the watch in fright and told Ursula about the mysterious find.

On the same day, and also behind Philip's voluminous encyclopaedia of music, a plastic bag with a dozen battery-operated razors came to light. Philip had the peculiar habit of almost always forgetting to pack a razor for his worldwide trips. When checking in at the airport it would occur to him that this important utensil for ensuring his perfect appearance in public had been left behind in the bathroom in Hamilton Terrace. And once again he felt obliged to buy a substitute before boarding. He also decided on one that was not too expensive, was battery-powered and made for travelling. Back home again in London he would hide the appliances in a plastic bag and hope that Ursula would not discover them. She might, in her good-natured way, which he often could not fathom, have the audacity to laugh at his impressive collection of memory lapses or worryingly early signs of forgetfulness. The Korean home help belonged to a Christian community and took the perfectly functioning appliances to a home for lonely fellow citizens, who, being elderly, would also mislay one thing or another and then not be able to remember, for example, where they had last used their razor.

Ursula's mother travelled back home after the wedding celebrations. Her opinion of her son-in-law did not change, and all the people in his, and undoubtedly Ursula's, friendship circles, with their affection for the newly-wed couple, seemed to her more and more peculiar and suspicious. Could she and her husband have been caught in a trap, taken in by a nasty plot, when ordering her yearlong separation from the trumpeter before giving herself body and soul to him? There was that, to her, completely strange sense of humour of this Englishman, who was admittedly a master of the trumpet; always that superior smile in his eyes, which were actually not that unpleasant. Some time later, during one of the never-ending arguments about his undesirable family-in-law, Philip would call Ursula's mother an obstinate peasant's wife from the Swiss mountains. Ursula was furious. How on earth was this admittedly smartly dressed city dweller to know what a peasant's wife from the Swiss mountains was like? And, what was more, she was a forerunner of the fight for women's right to vote in that country dominated by men until 1971. It was the men who could not see beyond the ends of their noses! One of them, who only knew those mountains from picture postcards, was clearly an even more obstinate mule. Yes, indeed: she was a peasant's wife, without a farm. He thought he had found a good term of abuse, but peasant's wife was not one. Not for her: legacy-hunter as he was, he would never get anywhere near to matching her, with her money, earned by hard work and competent dealings. And who knows, perhaps the marriage had not been lawfully completed.

Philip would have liked to have married in a country church, with bells rung by a real bell-ringer. For administrative and probably timing reasons the only possibility remained London and the church considered its oldest: St Bartholomew the Great, one of the most beautiful of God's houses in London. Also, Philip knew the priest. But one could only be married there after having been a member of the parish for a certain length of time, and had declared publicly that one would make the bond for life, the man with a woman, the woman with a man. If anyone had an objection to the union, they had the right to vote against it. After a discussion with 'Ursi' and the people in charge of St Bartholomew the Great, it was agreed that Philip, during the designated time, was to deposit a suitcase with personal effects with the sacristan of the church in order to establish residency.

Oh well, in Switzerland, those who wanted to marry were also put into transparent boxes for a few weeks. Raising objections, in case the wish for legal partnership did not meet with everyone's approval, was common practice. Tricks were ruled out. Who would want to be cheating when saying the yes-word, till death us do part.

Walter and Maria Strebi-Erni did not investigate further and, having disinherited their daughter, left things at that. Might they ever have considered that such a dual-nationality marriage was in danger of breaking up? Here there was a direct democracy in which women could only voice their opinions within the family and only with the approval of a male authority, and over there there was the complicated system of a constitutional monarchy with a parliament consisting of a lower and an upper house.

Later, Ursula's and Philip's marriage proved itself so robust that neither foreign currencies, fine linguistic differences, diverging culinary habits, cancelled postbus services via Grimsel, Furka and Susten, neither the Föhn nor the fog, nor the London tube (that took a bit of getting used to), were reasons why one could not sit down together for afternoon tea and apple crumble, or yearn for a fondue. Money was no longer important. Then, even if her parents had revised their inheritance decision, neither Ursula nor Philip would have accepted it.

But this has to be said too: in 1964 Ursula's father helped her to acquire the house in Hamilton Terrace with a small loan. Altogether the purchase price was £23,000, a steep price at that time. Today's price for a property in this, one of the most expensive areas of London, is in the millions. Many millions.

Philip Jones died in the year 2000. Since then the value of the house has risen further and exorbitantly. Accordingly Ursula has made changes to her will. To the last penny her assets will go where music, its creators and interpreters, will profit from them generously. Prizes will be created, cultural institutions will be catered for with considerable sums. It takes one's breath away to hear Ursula confidentially listing what will be done with the millions, once she is no longer living in the house complete with its memorial plaque to Philip.

What is more than admirable is what this once disinherited, in the eyes of her friends most deeply humiliated woman wants to achieve with her money. To think what she could have acquired for herself! She, who for her whole life was as modest as modest can be, only allowed herself a few long but culturally or archaeologically necessary trips, innumerable concerts, operas, theatre visits, always making sure not to go over the top with the tickets, flights and other fares, visits to restaurants and buying clothes. Of course, with her untiring urge to get things done, and with Philip's status in the musical world, she could have had anything she wanted. To profit from the fact that the house, for which she and her husband had worked very hard until it was fully paid for, gained in value to an almost indecent degree without any input on her part, seemed to her simply immoral. But leave it to the state? Ursula had no sympathy for the Robin-Hood moral either. For a while now an immigrant family from Iran is living in the mews, the coachman's house on the far side of the garden. When the husband from a traditional carpet-making family wanted to open a carpet-cleaning shop and came up against fierce resistance by the bank, Ursula was straight onto it; not without due consideration, although some acquaintances in the well-to-do neighbourhood accused her of a lack of it. As long as the status of the Iranian family is not altered by any unforeseen circumstances, the coach house will become their property. Not as a gift. The rent being paid over the years will count towards the purchase.

'Back then I joined the demonstrations when more than a million Londoners went on the streets to protest against George W. Bush's and Tony Blair's Iraq War. Proudly I held high a 'No-War' banner. The protest was ignored. But now if I can help a family in need gain a decent life style, then this peaceful protest against misery in this world will perhaps be a bit more tangible and lasting.'

When Ursula's mother died at the age of 107 in 2014, her whole fortune was passed over to the Maria und Walter Strebi-Erni Trust with Ursula's full agreement. Ursula took over as chairman, reorganised the board of trustees, and kept her activities in London quite separate from those of the Trust, which are mostly limited to Central Switzerland.

Ursula is committed to the Lucerne Theatre, the Lucerne Festival, the Lucerne Symphony Orchestra, and tries to take into consideration the requests of as many other smaller cultural groups as possible.

In Lucerne Ursula is easily forgiven for a trait of Englishness that she can never quite suppress. In the context of the concert cycles of the Gesellschaft für Kammermusik Marianischer Saal, Luzern, she has for many years been bringing to Switzerland brilliant young musicians she has discovered, and the Lucerne Symphony Orchestra, with its Konzert für Rising Stars, is an important institution as an international platform for soloists at the beginning of great careers. Since 2017 The Strebi-Erni Trust is the main sponsor of the debut series at the Lucerne Festival. Also, since 2017 the Philip-Jones Prize is donated for the best brass player at the Lucerne Conservatoire. In addition the Trust awards several prizes in memory of Ursula's father, Walter Strebi.

Ursula's unerring sense for exceptional talents is just as indisputable as the fact that she works hard for her protégés with a nigh on unrelenting commitment, shies away neither from her conviction nor from giving up time in order to smooth the roughest path to the top of the pyramid.

'I'd rather do without a reception with dull speeches, champagne and delicious canapés, than not to be able to offer another important venue for a tour. Music is not a material luxury but a spiritual one.'

# Chapter 8

## *Piggy Bank*

Ursula is not an early riser, yet a night owl needing little sleep: the result of decades working in the music business, and her marriage to a musician. She easily and quickly accustomed herself to the working time of people who, every evening and for the sake of others, become artists, stand on a stage, play in concert halls, make music in orchestra pits in time with singers; in all, achieving great things for the people in the audience who just wish to forget the everyday, to switch their batteries to stand-by, to lean back and enjoy what they have paid for at the box office.

After her late-night bath ritual and a few hours' sleep, Ursula gets up at half past seven in the morning and makes herself a strong cup of coffee with a good old single-cup filter. The coffee must be freshly ground, and from a coffee plantation known to pay its workers properly and where no child labour is tolerated. A fruit juice, a bowl of muesli with fresh fruit. If the phone rings before nine it is not answered, except if she knows that her representative at the Trust in Lucerne is ringing an hour early because of the time difference. There is a lot to discuss. To secure its assets and revenue the Trust is having an architecturally, ecologically and economically designed but superior complex built outside Lucerne. The letting started off well, then suffered an inexplicable slump. The low mortgage interest rate had attracted more purchasers than tenants. But rents guarantee a regular income out of which the ever-increasing applications can be fulfilled more fairly than with a one-off payment that does not yield interest or might even yield negative interest.

And then there is the real estate in Zug which, due to conflict with neighbours, is less a material than an ideational mortgage. There are many vehement discussions about whether selling would be the solution.

A time has to be fixed for a meeting with advisers for dealing with a whole pile of funding requests. Ursula's engagements diary is a permanent problem. For obvious reasons the meeting has to take place in Lucerne. Happy as the advisers would be to come to London, their travelling expenses would be enough to cover one or another funding request. 'What on earth have I landed myself with?' Ursula asks, suppressing a deep sigh. Well, the Trust exists, has to be kept going, and Lucerne does not lie just around the corner like Lord's Cricket Ground. A suitable date is found.

The canton of Lucerne has once more made it clear that all this spending of money cannot continue. Everywhere the red pen has to be applied: with education just as much as with culture, and just as rigorously with social as with health matters. The grant for the Lucerne Symphony Orchestra should be cut by half a million, which would set off a series of cuts by other benefactors. The streets, the whole construction industry and agriculture would soon be much more debated than culture and education. The governance of Lucerne is a regular men's club. More than an iron will to save money cannot be expected of the 'high-up gentlemen'.

If it is about music, you cannot mess with Ursula. Her, or rather her parents' Trust has, with the benefactors and sponsors, led to the expansion of the orchestra, and with it, a clearly audible improvement in quality. Ursula hears alarm bells ringing.

Before having to buy a few things for lunch, she books the flight from London City Airport to Zurich. Coming for lunch are the founder of Streetwise Opera and a further member of the board of this inspired institution for re-socialising the homeless. The famous cheese pie à la Ursula will be served up. It is not far to the small supermarket in Clifton Road. In the past, on her way to the little 'village' with its two shops, a pub and a florist, Ursula might meet up with neighbours for a short chat. Sometimes this made her forget what she had gone out for, but it meant that she caught up with a lot of private news and the gossip and scandal of the neighbourhood. They exchanged news and fixed a longer get-together. There were the Johnsons, the Leavers, the Strangs, the Mackerrases, the Noakes, the Drummonds. Nowadays only she and the Strangs are left. The houses of her favourite neighbours have been sold, gutted, and fitted out with everything needed for trendy luxury living. All very rich people, or at least so they seem, the new owners, some of whom sell up again having just moved in; whereupon the new owner repeats the gutting procedure, has an underground swimming pool built under the garden, using monstrous machines that make the whole district shake.

Nick and Deliah who, after two accidents that left them with permanent injuries, could no longer keep up their house, which they had filled with art from top to bottom, sold the property below the market price to an exceedingly friendly family with children who would have been better for St John's Wood than the anonymous business people from all parts of the world. Nick and Deliah moved to the country, near to their children. The new owners were never seen. After the legally prescribed time the house was sold on at an outrageous price.

Edgware Road, with its almost oriental Church Street Market, is also not what it used to be, growing more and more into a slightly inferior kind of Oxford Street with innumerable Arabic restaurants.

Matt Peacock, the founder of Streetwise Opera, is standing with another board member at the front door in Hamilton Terrace. In the dining room the table is laid. In the centre a candlestick with lighted candles. The glasses are very old. If one drinks a toast, they make a wonderful sound. Philip was a great admirer and connoisseur of these 'musical' glasses. The cheese pie is delicious.

'Swiss cheese?'

'No. Cheddar from Tesco's down in the village.'

It is all about a new project, to start a new production with homeless people. This time not in a church: an opera of our time. The globalisation, the unusual management and the excessive influence of the omnipresent adviser are to be like a red thread going through the opera. The motto: 'Something for nothing'. The slogan, conveying everything and nothing: 'Locateco Solutions'. The musical direction of the project will be by composer and conductor Duncan Ward. Duncan, discovered and consistently promoted by Ursula, is the rising star in the classical music scene.

This meeting is about performance venues. The British Film Institute on the South Bank would be ideal. A connection has already been established. Getting funds is in hand. Streetwise Opera has been described by the Prime Minister as a pioneering social and artistic organisation. Soon money will not be the main topic at meetings: the artistic side could be more heavily weighted. Again it is Ursula's diary that determines the next meeting. 'That's Ursula. She belongs to us all.' Without her, all briefly considered ideas would be shoved to the back of the cupboard. How does she find the time, why does that flow of ideas never dry up?

In the garden there is a little stone sculpture with a birdbath; probably a secret fount of youth. An archaeology friend rings up whose work on Mexican deities is to be published. Could Ursula possibly give an introduction and speech in her honour at the launch? Gods are not Ursula's speciality, but she knows an emeritus professor who would certainly be glad to go public again.

A group of music-lovers from the DRS2 Kulturclub (now Radio SRF2 Kulturclub) is coming to London. Ursula is asked to organise the cultural programme. Concerts, an opera, an evening at the theatre and a visit to Glyndebourne are planned and almost all already set in train. Only Glyndebourne has not yet got the go ahead. The tickets seem rather expensive to her colleague in Switzerland who is in charge of the trip. Ursula will get in touch with the executive chairman and grandson of the founder of the exclusive country opera house: 'a close friend.' Ursula will try. She cannot promise anything, but if Ursula promises to try something, it is as good as done.

The manager of the Young Classical Artists Trust (YCAT) agency rings up. It is about a young musician, a brass player. She asks for Ursula's opinion. Anyone who is looked after by YCAT has already got a foot on the career ladder. Over a period of three to five years the young people are taken under the wing of the trust and passed on to other similar institutions until they are finally standing on their own two feet in the most famous concert halls in the world. The Belcea and Sacconi quartets were not only looked after by YCAT: Ursula also had a hand in that. Ursula gives her opinion of the young brass player. Perhaps he will be taken on by YCAT: a recommendation from Ursula is half the battle.

For an archaeological trip to Mexico there are still a lot of things to sort out. Not all the participants will be flying together to Mexico City. Ursula does not wish to give the impression that she alone is deciding on the route and the highlights to be visited. But in the end everything does fall to her, and her fingers start working on the keyboard of her computer. Her fingers are troubling her. A difficult operation on her neck vertebrae has resulted in a noticeable handicap. 'Not worth talking about. The surgeons in the paraplegic centre in Nottwil did their best. The main thing is that I can walk straight again, perhaps even ski again.'

When, a few years ago, Ursula not only got a new right knee but also a new left one, after only a few months rest she climbed the Allalinhorn in the canton of Valais. She does not say how high this mountain is: one can imagine it. After the knee operation and a fall, which could have had horrific consequences, she promised a friend never to run for a bus again. And then she did go and miss her footing getting onto a double-decker bus. Her knee hurt, and she was astonished that a joint could hurt when it was made of an insensitive alloy of titanium and plastic.

Her wish to learn how to tap dance some time in her life gets stronger from year to year. She has long since found out where one can buy the right shoes and protective cover for the floor, and once even visited the right shop.

A phone call to the Royal Opera House, Covent Garden confirms what she has suspected: all performances of the highly praised opera *Oedipe* by Georges Enescu are sold out. However, it is always possible to get returns if one queues early enough. So off to Covent Garden it is. Hunger can be satisfied in the interval. A change of clothes is not necessary. Perhaps a better jacket. Not even in the Royal Opera House is one's attire the most important thing anymore. One should feel comfortable and not have one's pleasure at the sounds and sights of a great work spoilt by the constraints of fashion.

In the underground Ursula tells the story of a young man who had a cultural scholarship from the Landis & Gyr Foundation. He had not been in London long when by chance he walked past the Festival Hall. He stood in awe in front of the mighty bust of Nelson Mandela and then saw in a showcase behind it that the City of Birmingham Symphony Orchestra was playing Mahler's first symphony under a certain Simon Rattle. The scholar was wearing jeans and a black T-shirt. He bought one of the last available tickets for a seat in the gallery behind the stage, and asked at the box office about the dress code for the Festival Hall. The lady in the ticket office bent forwards a little, looked the man up and down, smiled and said that he did not need to change.

Once again, music should never be a material luxury.

While queuing for possible ticket returns Ursula meets a friend. Should she be able to get hold of a ticket he would invite her to a glass of wine and some fine canapés in the interval. Michael Conroy lives around the corner from the residence of the Swiss Embassy. His flat is so big that house concerts can be given there. Ursula 'procures' the musicians for Michael, he concerns himself with the well-being of the soloists and guests. Sol Gabetta, Alison Balsom, Miloš Karadaglić and Ksenija Sidorova are among the many artists who owe great thanks to Ursula as well as Michael.

A lady emerges from behind her computer in the box office at the Royal Opera House Covent Garden and offers Ursula two returned tickets. Not quite the cheapest. Well, so what. Enescu's great opera *Oedipe* will be worth it. Sung in French after Sophocles, so Ursula will be able to follow it.

An overwhelming set immediately captures the audience. The plot is more or less well known. Who does not know the story of the innocent guilty? Who has never grappled with the Oedipus complex? Enescu also includes Sophocles' later *Oedipus at Colonus*, and shows the redemption of the hero. The production and the soloists are convincing. The British bass Sir John Tomlinson is brilliant in the role of the blind seer Tiresias. Sarah Connolly presents her role no less outstandingly. No one is below par. The orchestra is on the ball up to the very last note. A great evening. The glass of wine and delicious canapés are consumed almost in silence, thanks to the impact of the first half. One should not devalue great art with chit-chat.

Overwhelmed, Ursula stands under the glass dome of the Floral Hall. And now? A bit further down towards the Thames and near the English National Opera, Ursula offers an invitation to her club, The Two Brydges. One of the narrowest alleys in London leads to a nondescript door. One press on the bell, a woman's voice, and Ursula gives her name. The door opens. The entrance is even narrower than the alley. A confined and extremely steep staircase leads up to where a young, very pleasant lady greets Ursula with unaffected warmth. It is actually too late for dinner, but for Ursula an exception will of course be made. There is still a lovely glass of wine and a light, mixed salad with delicious seafood to be had. Every now and then one has to match spiritual artistic pleasure with the pleasure of the tongue. A good meal, a good wine in friendly society can do more than just round off a visit to a concert, theatre or museum. One can comment on Enescu's *Oedipe* with many positive opinions, although Stravinsky's *Oedipus Rex* can affect one more deeply with the music alone. The conciliatory ending that allows some hope, seems bland. That the recently experienced opera inevitably leads to a mild argument about the Oedipus conflict or complex, evoked by Freud, somehow affects the music still ringing in one's ears.

So what, says Ursula; with her it would be an Elektra complex. In a redemptive way, she too had cleared things up with her mother. Leniency of old age? Of the mother or the daughter? Of both. No, 107 years old like her mother Ursula on no account wants to be: the total dependency on others, loss of hearing, almost going blind, not being able to control one's whole organism with one's own energy. For Uncle Hans, who became almost as old and to the end was blessed with an untiring creative urge, old age was probably more bearable. Was it not once said somewhere that 100,000 are enough for a politician? A hundred, reckons Ursula, is more than enough for a human being.

The fact that the wages of executive members of the town council have risen massively since there was the question of limiting them to 100,000 Swiss francs, is quite out of proportion to the life expectancy of a human being. And it is undoubtedly a privilege if a wife or a husband is well over 80 years old and still full of energy, making many a younger man green with envy. Others might call it a gift of God. Once one is aware of this privilege, day by day everything else becomes less important. For Ursula it is an irrefutable fact that one should be thankful for this gift if it is combined with a selfless commitment to people who still have their whole lives in front of them.

So, off home again. There are still letters to write and minutes to read that have come in the post. Ursula wants to be armed for the telephone conference with the Trust's board members far off in Switzerland, set for tomorrow morning. It is past midnight. Long since. The tube trains are not running any more. It is only a short walk to the night buses at Trafalgar Square. But it has been a long day. If need be one could always afford a taxi. To sit in the back of a black cab, especially at night, like that time in King Richard's midnight-blue Rolls-Royce Phantom Six, is a pleasure, perhaps in a way only Londoners can enjoy. The taxi drivers know the nicest, most exciting routes to all destinations, and are well known for not doing any expensive detours.

Ursula knows the story of an author who, out there in the East End, got it into his head to explore the murders of Jack the Ripper, possibly to dramatize them, to turn them into a radio play. When the connoisseur of the monstrous happenings of 1888 got into a taxi after a reception in the ballroom of Grosvenor House, Park Lane, to get to his modest flat in Whitechapel, the driver asked him what business he had in Whitechapel after a visit to one of the most expensive hotels. Not quite up to understanding the cockney of this seemingly genuine East Ender, the passenger tried to explain that he was working on an account of Jack the Ripper's misdeeds. By then they had reached Liverpool Street Station; the driver turned off his meter and drove the astonished passenger, in his dark suit, white shirt and black bow tie, to every location of the murders of prostitutes in 1888, and knew much more about the social conditions of those days than the 'connoisseur' had read up.

Ursula especially remembered one important detail. The taxi driver is said to have mentioned that after the Germans had bombed Buckingham Palace, the Queen Mother had, on visiting the East End, said that the attack had done some good for the Crown: now they, the privileged of the relatively spared West, could look the much worse affected people of the East End in the eye. If Queen Victoria had had a similar consideration for the residents of London east of the Tower, Jack the Ripper might not have found the fertile ground for his hideous deeds.

What a shame that the evening, with the grandiose opera and the very late little dinner, was too far advanced, bearing in mind the one or two urgent matters to be dealt with, otherwise she would now have been ready to go to the east and experience the horrors of Whitechapel. Well, Enescu had already made cold sweat run down her back. Instead of Trafalgar Square Ursula suggested Piccadilly. Then one was already going in the right direction, and there were buses to Oxford Circus, where one could change and go directly home. She knew all the alternatives. She was the owner of a Freedom Pass, that ingenious acquisition from which all taxpaying London residents over 65 can profit. Journeys on all public transport in all zones, free of charge. Over a whole year, that amounted to a good thousand pounds. Anyone who did not take advantage of this privilege had only themselves to blame. At night too. Ursula insists that it goes absolutely without saying that the buses are a safe mode of transport. She is not being naïve, as some of her older and more easily frightened friends keep trying to tell her. Naturally she knows that there are plenty of potential criminals around, thefts are the order of the day, elderly ladies have their handbags snatched. One winter, when several centimetres of slush lay on Hamilton Terrace and it was still snowing so hard that the windscreen wipers gave up, Lady Mackerras was forced to roll down both side windows when she parked in front of her house. At that moment a barefaced young man thrust his long arm and even longer fingers into the car, grabbed the handbag lying on the passenger seat and disappeared before the petite lady, fierce though she could be, had time to do anything about it. There was great indignation throughout St John's Wood. There was more talk about Neighbourhood Watch. The police invited people to information evenings. The consequence was an increasing feeling of insecurity among the elderly: they retreated more and more behind their barred doors and windows.

Once, when Ursula and Philip were both away on a concert tour, a well informed thief climbed over the roof and through the window into Philip's studio and took possession of the valuable collection of old clocks, anything else of value and all of Ursula's Cashmere pullovers. After that, those windows, which had been considered secure, were also barred.

Instead of being afraid of any passenger who sits next to her on a night bus, thinking him to be a scoundrel, Ursula starts up a conversation with these people, who certainly are only interested in getting home at night without any bother. Ursula can tell many good stories about such encounters. From Charing Cross to St John's Wood Road, she once talked with an elderly Arab lady about the hijab, the burka and Ramadan, and, without showing it, was amused by the funny, though absolutely comprehensible English. The lady thanked her for the conversation with a spontaneous hug and wished Ursula a 'good knife'.

Back home in Hamilton Terrace, before the work still to be done and the nightly bath and going to bed, Ursula fancies a little glass of Baselbieter Kirsch. One can talk best in the kitchen when the whole house and its surroundings are dark. She takes 25 pounds in notes out of her purse and puts the money into a special envelope. It used to be a piggy bank. Probably the taxi would only have cost £22. To do good one should not be stingy. Since she possesses a Freedom Pass and uses it avidly, she puts the money that she would have used for the more comfortable taxi rides into this piggy bank and has financed young, talented musicians for years. Perhaps, on those almost nightly journeys, the thought of the money saved covers her with a protective shield and makes her invulnerable to crooked intentions.

# Photo Gallery

1 Ursula Jones in her living room in Hamilton Terrace.

2 Maria Strebi-Erni and Walter Strebi, Ursula's parents, generous hosts of innumerable guests.

3 Ursula in her Uncle Hans Erni's studio.

4 Ursula in her mother's arms.

5 Ursula's maternal grandfather, engineer on the
paddle steamer 'Uri' of the Lake Lucerne fleet, and artist.

6 Glamour at the stage door in the old Kunsthaus in Lucerne.
Ursula, Wilhelm Furtwängler, Maria Strebi and an
unknown admirer of the great conductor.

7 Daniel Barenboim, Jacqueline du Pré, Pinchas Zukerman, Zubin Mehta, Ernest Fleischmann.

8 Pillars of the English Chamber Orchestra: Ursula,
Quintin Ballardie and Daniel Barenboim.

9 'Brass is my passion!' Ursula and her husband Philip Jones.

*We are happy to announce our marriage which was celebrated at the church of St. Bartholomew the Great, in the City of London, on August 1st, 1956.*

*Philip M. Jones*                                        *Ursula Strebi*

*2, Mansfield Mews, Harley Street, London, W.1.*

10 Ursula Strebi and Philip Jones announce their wedding, not approved of by all. Drawing by Hans Erni.

86

11 Ursula and Philip Jones celebrate one of their
many wedding anniversaries in Morcote.

12 Always a gentleman from top to toe.
Philip Jones on a tour in Germany.

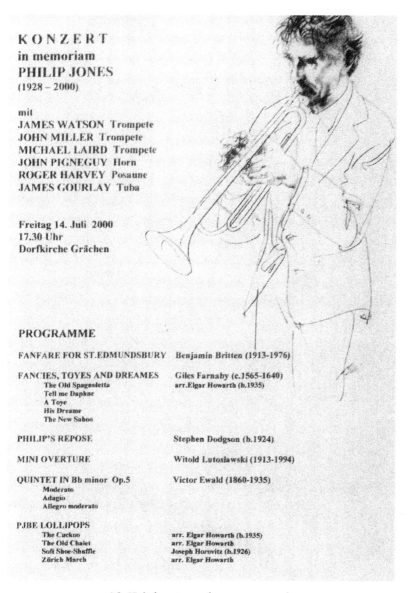

KONZERT
in memoriam
PHILIP JONES
(1928 – 2000)

mit
JAMES WATSON  Trompete
JOHN MILLER  Trompete
MICHAEL LAIRD  Trompete
JOHN PIGNEGUY  Horn
ROGER HARVEY  Posaune
JAMES GOURLAY  Tuba

Freitag 14. Juli 2000
17.30 Uhr
Dorfkirche Grächen

PROGRAMME

| | |
|---|---|
| FANFARE FOR ST.EDMUNDSBURY | Benjamin Britten (1913-1976) |
| FANCIES, TOYES AND DREAMES<br>The Old Spagnoletta<br>Tell me Daphne<br>A Toye<br>His Dreame<br>The New Saboo | Giles Farnaby (c.1565-1640)<br>arr.Elgar Howarth (b.1935) |
| PHILIP'S REPOSE | Stephen Dodgson (b.1924) |
| MINI OVERTURE | Witold Lutoslawski (1913-1994) |
| QUINTET IN Bb minor  Op.5<br>Moderato<br>Adagio<br>Allegro moderato | Victor Ewald (1860-1935) |
| PJBE LOLLIPOPS<br>The Cuckoo<br>The Old Chalet<br>Soft Shoe-Shuffle<br>Zürich March | arr. Elgar Howarth (b.1935)<br>arr. Elgar Howarth<br>Joseph Horovitz (b.1926)<br>arr. Elgar Howarth |

13 'Là-haut sur la montagne'.
The memorial concert for Philip Jones in Grächen.

14 Villa Melitta, the house in Morcote, where Ursula's young musicians often perform.

15 Ursula with the three flautists of the Tempest Flute Trio, in Davos.

16 The conductor and composer Duncan Ward with Philip's 'Büchel' at the chalet Chems near Grächen.

17 Ursula with Benjamin Britten during a rehearsal in Blythburgh Church.

18 The singer Willard White names Ursula as Honorary Member of the Northern College of Music in Manchester.

19 HM Queen Elizabeth II honours Ursula Jones for her great services to music.

**Elizabeth the Second,** by the Grace of God of the
United Kingdom of Great Britain and Northern Ireland and of Her
other Realms and Territories Queen, Head of the Commonwealth,
Defender of the Faith and Sovereign of the Most Excellent Order of the
British Empire to Our trusty and well beloved Ursula Jones

Greeting

**Whereas** We have thought fit to nominate and appoint you to be
an Ordinary Officer of the Civil Division of Our said Most Excellent Order
of the British Empire

**We do** by these presents grant unto you the Dignity of an Ordinary
Officer of Our said Order and hereby authorise you to have hold and enjoy
the said Dignity and Rank of an Ordinary Officer of Our aforesaid Order
together with all and singular the privileges thereunto belonging or
appertaining.

**Given** at Our Court at Saint James's under Our Sign Manual
and the Seal of Our said Order this Twelfth day of June 2010 in the
Fifty-ninth year of Our Reign.

By the Sovereign's Command.

Grand Master

Grant of the Dignity of an Ordinary Officer of the Civil Division
of the Order of the British Empire
to Ursula, Mrs. Jones


20 Officer of the Order of the British Empire (OBE).
The document presented by the Queen.

93

21 Philip Jones with his alphorn on Hublen, Valais.

22 Ursula and Philip Jones duo at the chalet Chems.

23 Ursula's new passion: in tandem with Robert paragliding from the peaks into the valley.

24 Ursula Jones and her neighbour and friend, Sherry Johnson
on the summit of Kilimanjaro.

25 A long life dedicated to music. Ursula Jones in the
Philip Jones Room in Trinity Laban Conservatoire of Music.

# Chapter 9

## *Bad News*

The three years with the Philharmonia Orchestra were for Ursula more than an apprenticeship. The comparison with the deep end into which she jumped, neither due to necessity nor to being pushed, is not a very good one as she was a good swimmer and still is, even in heavy seas. An example of this was a planned journey that she did not wish to postpone shortly after a cancer operation. She trusted the doctors of the Lucerne Kantonspital and assumed that anyone who was discharged from that hospital was naturally considered to have made a full recovery.

Lady Mackerras, her slightly older neighbour, who shortly before Ursula also had to be operated on for breast cancer, but who was on her feet astonishingly quickly and active as ever, confessed to her husband to seeing the world rather more darkly since losing a breast. She felt as if the paints on her palette, intended for cheerful pictures, had dried out. The great conductor, Sir Charles Mackerras, took his wife into his arms, sang to the tune of an old Australian children's song: 'Ain't it a pity, she's only one titty.' Whenever she got the feeling that she was no longer an adequate wife, Judy, without the words, hummed to herself Sir Charles's perhaps rather frivolous little song. Certainly it would never have occurred to her to dismiss Sir Charles's well intentioned but rash consolation as out-dated sexism. She liked the tune, but rather without the words.

Ursula travelled to the mountains with the wound from her operation not fully healed. Her kind neighbour and friend, Sherry, accompanied her and changed her bandage when necessary. Then, bandage free, Ursula was off on an archaeological trip to Turkey. Here she could not be dissuaded from jumping from the sailing boat into the deep blue water and swimming until she could no longer hear the cries of warning.

In the world of music there were storms mainly in half-full or, according to one's point of view, in half-empty teacups, or perhaps wine or schnapps glasses. If anyone went overboard it was Ursula who was at the ready with a lifebelt.

When she had got well into working with the Philharmonia Orchestra and began to get promising hints, she entertained justified hopes of being promoted from secretary to manager. But Walter Legge was firmly against Ursula and favoured a less dynamic woman over the lively Swiss one. Ursula was absolutely convinced that personal animosity or rather her relationship with her parents regarding the unacceptable Philip Jones were the reason why the owner of the orchestra and good friend of her father had passed her over.

'Well, I shall just have to start my own orchestra.'

Ursula's not very serious defiance at first overlapped with the founding of a London branch of the art club 'Kunstkreis', established in Lucerne by Herr Schweizer. High quality art prints were available to the public. Nowadays one might not give much more than a weary smile at people who want to hang their Van Goghs, Matisses, Mirós and Kandinskys in their flats. Under Ursula's leadership in London, the art club became known as International Art Club Editions, functioning by means of subscription and mail order. In Mansfield Mews, where Ursula and Philip were living at that time, Ursula's widowed mother-in-law was also living, next door on the first floor, as well as the bank clerk Charles Peters, an enthusiastic opera lover and admirer and friend of Maria Callas. On the ground floor International Art Club Editions developed into a blossoming enterprise with Schweizer's recipe for success with investments. The English Chamber Orchestra also became an institution in Mansfield Mews. Ursula's dream of her own orchestra was heading more rapidly than expected towards realisation. She had never been a passionate businesswoman (and now, despite her immense responsibility for the Strebi-Erni Trust, probably never will be), and she probably foresaw the decline in demand for art prints, so she sold the whole business after three years and concentrated exclusively on her orchestra and the career of her husband, Philip Jones.

Quintin Ballardie, a viola player who had been in charge of the Goldsbrough Orchestra, a chamber orchestra of a very high standard, was on the look out for an experienced orchestral secretary, and found her in Ursula. To his astonishment she applied so much initiative to the business that it sometimes made him giddy. Goldsbrough: no one abroad could pronounce this name. Should the experienced manager give way? Absolutely, yes. The young woman was at home in many languages. With her a crucial step could be taken: what Quintin Ballardie dreamt of could be achieved. The world was now much more open to music than it had been in the immediate post-war years; and English orchestras were known throughout the empire, even if the grand, political influence was beginning to fray at the edges.

English Chamber Orchestra? Quite simple but clear, and actually new. Married though she was to an aspiring English trumpeter, what this young Swiss woman thought up, an experienced impresario would quite happily claim for himself. A cunning fox like Quintin Ballardie knew better than most that even while this Philip Jones stirred up and dominated the brass scene completely, his wife would be forming strong connections with great people like Geza Anda, Karl Richter, Rafael Kubelík and other luminaries.

Ursula Jones and Quintin Ballardie made a successful duo, even if there were some tense moments. She tracked down the soloists and conductors, engaged them, and he guaranteed the best orchestral players available on the market. It was not by chance that the phenomenal cellist, Jacqueline du Pré played with Daniel Barenboim conducting from the piano, that Karl Richter was in the team, that Pinchas Zukerman was turning into the second 'devil's violinist'. Superb flautists, Anita Lasker-Wallfisch, the cellist from Auschwitz, many young people, great interpreters, all mastering their métier. A golden age was dawning. Ursula gave the rightly praised pianist, Daniel Barenboim, the chance to try conducting. Often such changes did not turn out well: the two activities were like chalk and cheese. For that, an orchestra was the best seismograph. And under Daniel Barenboim it displayed a completely new strength. The ECO had found its maestro.

The du Pré-Barenboim team could hardly be reined in. Both inquisitive and young, both passionate, he only marginally interested in English music, she not too familiar with Wagner. Fascinating friction points occurred, which, with their unconditionally passionate devotion to each other, always led to new heights. Would the ECO have gained its world fame without these two geniuses? Without the ECO, would Daniel Barenboim and Jacqueline du Pré have fetched the stars from heaven, which, quite justifiably, they had reached for?

Ursula's ECO was not a talent factory. Some of the most gifted orchestral players had got together thanks to Quintin Ballardie, and Ursula fashioned the collection of self-confident instrumentalists and individualists into an orchestra.

That Ursula played a part in Daniel Barenboim's career is evident from the gratitude shown by the great conductor and pianist. When Ursula's mother was 90 and Ursula and Barenboim met at the Lucerne Festival, he spontaneously offered to give a private concert for Maria Strebi's 100th birthday. Two years before the event she reminded him of his promise. With great regret he discovered that he would be on a tour in South America at the time in question. 'But how about we count the day of her birth as the first birthday?' On the 99th birthday of Ursula's mother Daniel Barenboim travelled to Lucerne and played more than just a serenade in the Marianische Saal. It was a real concert, performed with great passion, and received tremendous applause and included many encores.

Ursula was completely taken up with her new task. She became the ECO, she alone organised the concerts, fixed the orchestral players, planned the tours, and above all she had to make sure the ECO was financially secure. It is difficult to imagine how a single person managed to keep an orchestra business going. There were no photocopiers. If something had to be duplicated it was a case of carbon paper between the sheets. Much was handwritten and repeatedly crossed out, rubbed out, added to. The telephone was the most important method of communication. A hand was constantly reaching for the receiver. It was word of mouth that counted: everywhere. Otherwise everything would have gone down the drain.

At 89 Ursula still could not rest and, after happily resolved problems, was always and everywhere available where even the best-organised institutions had reached their limits. This must have been due to the ECO, the International Arts Club and the West-End musicals, which were her schooling. A person who needs eight hours sleep, regular working hours and absolute financial security, would never cope with Ursula's workload. The manageress of the 'Two Brydges', with whom Ursula has very rapidly built up a lovely friendship, says that she has never met anyone who was always in such a good mood as Ursula. And this even after a day with a difficult computer problem, discussions with the executors of her will, a problem with a website that has not been updated, a lunch break that is too short, a traffic jam on the way into central London, almost missing the last entry time into an exhibition in the National Portrait Gallery, and a narrowly missed dinner at the club.

However, two days ago the clocks went back from summer to winter time. In Ursula's house the hot water and heating systems got muddled up. 'The bath water felt as if I was stepping into a stream at the snout of a glacier.' The English people around the table, descendants of Alpine pioneers, understood the shock, but 'if anyone had heard the words that escaped my lips at the desecration of my nightly bathing ritual, then their opinion of the "good-natured" Ursula would have to be radically altered.'

In 1974, after 14 years, she placed the management of the ECO into other hands, thus trusting someone else with 'her child'. It was only then that the musical world got a realistic picture of her occupation as a dynamic orchestral manager, an innovative, clever programme arranger and conscientious administrator of the ECO, which under her had become a legend. Children of her own were denied her. She has a strong personal attachment to the Chinese pianist, Miduo, and the trumpeter, Ying, whom she and Philip helped to get scholarships in London, and later to get established in Switzerland. She is proud of the 'foreign births' that she had set in train over the decades. However, she never wished to be a substitute mother. She knows this situation from both sides only too well. The fact that at exactly the right moment she got into the saddle and took hold of the reins to surmount and overcome vast, often impossibly high obstacles, made and makes her unendingly grateful. But to boast about her protégés' careers? Heavens, no. In her opinion no single person could ever be solely responsible for someone's career. 'A road on which one can travel fast is not built by one person.' Yet to count up all the many cultural projects that would not have happened without Ursula's untiring commitment, would be like the labour of Sisyphus. Innumerable personal, hand-written letters, private telephone calls. No phone call, e-mail, even when related to the same occasion, was a duplicate.

Ursula is convinced that in the enormous flood of events, nobody has a chance of the great, the real breakthrough, unless other, competent people support them. 'A hand-written letter is more effective than a thousand friends on Facebook or even more Twitter followers.' No wonder that Ursula's engagement diary looks like one belonging to a global CEO of a vast empire, close to burnout.

On the agenda for this afternoon is a meeting with lawyers about the settlement of her estate. Even if the proceeds from the property in Hamilton Terrace are divided into various legacies, the whole packet will first of all be put into the hands of the Royal Philharmonic Society. Ursula's will mainly takes up two sides of A4. To cater for all eventualities there are ten times more pages.

The evening chosen for a visit to the Wanamaker Theatre has been booked for quite a while. The invited friend, a star guitarist, one of whose hands needs a complete rest, has to cancel because of urgently needed therapy. So Ursula invites a friend whom she got to know on a tour in South America with the ECO. Alexandra was the wife of the British ambassador to Peru (later transferred to Vienna), now widowed and also an archaeologist late in life. She is just about to complete a comprehensive work on Peruvian stone sculptures of pre-Columbian times. She too is a lady of over 80 years with an unbroken, almost youthful vitality.

The piece by John Milton is enchanting. Ursula and Alexandra have a great time. The play is 400 years old and completely sold out. This discovery at the Wanamaker Playhouse, and seeing each other again, are cause for celebration.

Oh, yes, that time in Lima: the ECO on a grand tour, the enthusiastically received concert, the reception at the British embassy. And, since they were there, why not up to Machu Picchu as well. But the schedule was too complicated: the only possibility meant a flight to Cusco. The conquering English spirits had turned a deaf ear to the warnings about the very thin air above 4,000 metres. Half the orchestra collapsed. The dinner party at the British Embassy proved to be a great opportunity to satisfy a voracious appetite, also attributable to the thin air.

'Perhaps I was infected by Ursula's untiring interest in anything archaeological, by this woman who, beside her responsibility for the hungry and partly unbridled gang of musicians, used every moment to tackle the pre-Columbian times of Latin America.'

Alexandra thinks that Ursula's childhood wish, to dig up the treasures of long ago, was only properly revived on the concert tours with the ECO around the whole world. Everywhere where archaeology lured her, she, a layman, could hardly be held back and, with the best will in the world, could not understand why her musicians, in their free hours or days between concerts, did not want to accompany her to the ruins, to that extremely important 'rubbish' (as her parents would have called it). And yet she possessed such irresistible charm...

When the local guide in Cusco told her on the evening before their flight back to Lima that the aeroplane was not available because of other bookings, Ursula's first thought was that it was a joke. Then a music lover who knew how things worked in Peru let her know that, for better or worse, she would have to indicate to the official in charge that he would not be left empty-handed financially if he took steps to secure a flight. Ursula had no cash on her, and could not get any. She had no alternative but to flirt with this corrupt character until the last double bass was stowed in the hold and the orchestra was on board.

Another time, in Saloniki, an impresario and admirer who wanted to give the impression of being a generous patron, dared to invite Ursula to a candlelit tête-à-tête dinner in a cosy restaurant high up overlooking the sea. Ursula brought half the orchestra with her and, seeing that the table was only laid for two, pretended to have misunderstood the invitation. The ECO was never again invited to the festival in Saloniki. To make oneself unequivocally understood in foreign languages had always had its dangers, apologised the highly qualified translator.

Ursula, the sheltered girl from Lucerne, a city which during the summer was full of itself, with its important music festival, and then vanished from the world map of music centres, could seem misleadingly naïve, almost as naïve as one of her cellists at the station in Malmö, who, together with other members of the orchestra, saw in a kiosk for the first time a display of magazines with photos of naked women, and said in astonishment: 'My wife doesn't look like that at all.'

In the 1960s the world was for many of the orchestral musicians, as well as conductors, soloists and managers, still more or less all right. Signs that here and there some cracks were showing could be confidently overlooked. It was a pleasure to fly to Beirut and, under Raymond Leppard on two evenings in Baalbek, to play Purcell's *Fantasy in c minor,* Schönberg's *Verklärte Nacht*, Honegger's *Concerto da Camera*, Haydn's *Symphony no. 85*, Bach's *Brandenburg Concerto, No. 3*, Mozart's *Sinfonia Concertante*, Malcolm Arnold's flute concerto and Schubert's fifth symphony; and Ursula organised everything to everyone's satisfaction. Two days later Daniel Barenboim shone in Volos with Bartók's *Divertimento* and a Mozart piano concerto. Then flying via Saloniki to Zurich and, in Lucerne, again with Barenboim, there were truly great moments with Mozart, Bartók and Beethoven. A few days later the orchestra and Barenboim triumphed with Schubert, Mozart and Beethoven in Stresa.

The doors of the concert halls were more than just a crack open. Ursula travelled with her orchestra several times around the globe. Wherever the ECO performed, Quintin Ballardie's musicians and Ursula's conductors, soloists and programmes were euphorically received, and the critics surpassed themselves with eulogies.

And then, having reached the heights, the bad news: Ursula Strebi, the manager with an exceptionally strong hand yet extremely fine sensitivity, was leaving the ECO. In innumerable media reports and personal statements Ursula's well-considered step was regretted. Paul Sacher, who had as patron acquired many new compositions for the ECO, and treasured Ursula above everything, was appalled. The British Council, co-organisers of concert tours abroad, begged Ursula not to leave the world of music altogether. Isaac Stern identified Ursula with the ECO and was shaken by her resignation. From Buenos Aires Alejandro Sternenfeld let it be known that he was deeply saddened. The Settimane Musicali di Stresa went into mourning. The London Symphony Orchestra spoke of the end of a great era. In Barcelona the ECO could not be imagined without Ursula. The Association of British Orchestras begged Ursula always to remain accessible. The BBC sadly stated that it would never again be as wonderful in their studios as it had been with Ursula, who had always managed to resolve the most difficult situations. The concert halls of the London South Bank: the Royal Festival Hall, the Queen Elizabeth Hall and the Purcell Room, looked back to the time of all her glittering successes and moments of perfection that would be no more. Geza Anda wrote of an unparalleled fruitfulness and deeply personal relationship with her musicians. The *Daily Express* wrote of a personality whom one could always rely upon for help. The Senior Music Producer of the BBC wrote to Ursula that she would be missed everywhere you could think of: in the orchestra, in the concert hall and far beyond. The ninety-year-old Sir Robert Mayer, with the best will in the world, could not imagine the ECO without the soul of Ursula. The London Sinfonietta could express nothing but admiration for her. How lonely the music scene would be without her. At the Peter Stuyvesant Foundation they were rubbing their eyes at seeing Ursula's decision in print; and they were moist. EMI would deeply miss their co-operation with the wonderful Ursula. Her competence, highly praised by all, had brought success to every shared project. Pianist John Lewis could not imagine how such a fruitful co-operation with the ECO could function without Ursula's warm friendliness. The Chichester Festival asked Ursula always to remember the unique ECO concert with the great Jessye Norman: 'That was you, dearest Ursula.' The Macrobert Arts Centre of The University of Stirling declared that Ursula was responsible for one of the greatest eras of British music. The Konzertgesellschaft Wuppertal wrote: 'It was a wonderful time with you and your ECO. We will miss you very much and can only imagine with great difficulty how the gap that you have left will be filled. We knew that we could rely on you and your arrangement of concerts. Without in the smallest way trying to curry favour, you satisfied the taste of our demanding audiences with your programmes.' Ibbs and Tillet, the concert managers and impresarios of the Wigmore Hall, treasured the wonderfully artistic and business-like relationship. The top music programme manager of the BBC declared: 'What a pleasure it always was to be in harness with you, dear Ursula. I find it very difficult to imagine a close relationship with the ECO without you.' From Madrid came the sigh: 'What a pity no more having the pleasure to dealing with you' (sic). Music Ltd put the regret in a nutshell: 'Your enthusiasm, your unique diplomatic skill, your ever perfect work and your friendliness were beacons in the often stormy world of good music.' The Decca Record Company was quite simply and justifiably very sad at the loss. King's College, Cambridge expressed their regret thus: 'Ursula and the ECO. What a unique institution! And now?'

It was in Cambridge where Ursula for the first time fulfilled Daniel Barenboim's wish, and gave him the chance to try out being a conductor. For where this trial led to, for that grandiose journey, the world must thank Ursula Jones, who always heard the applause for her orchestra, her soloists and conductors quite unassumingly from somewhere in the audience.

# Chapter 10

## *Me and BB*

'Benjamin Britten, the bright star in the heavens of contemporary composers.' When that sort of admiration escapes Ursula's lips, there is also always a slightly well meaning yet sceptical laughter in her eyes; but never arrogant. Over more than 60 years in the music business Ursula has built up a huge range of insider knowledge; because of her profession, she has had to look for so long behind the scenes; was confronted by the daily lives of gifted musicians, the great and world renowned soloists, and shared their joy and sorrow. Much that is amusing and frivolous could be told. Anecdotes, much nonsense as well as crudeness, occurrences that were recounted by acquaintances about acquaintances of acquaintances, by friends of friends, and which still contained a vestige of what had actually happened. Or near enough.

There was the story about the brass player, who was well known as a soloist as well as a womanizer, with remarkable success; until one morning he woke up in a strange bed with a terrible thirst. On the bedside table lay only his watch, which he had taken off on the advice of the lady, who was still asleep. On the other side, where his conquest lay, he saw a glass of water. His completely dried up mouth would have led to a hideous throat-clearing had he not crept out of bed at the foot end, grabbed the glass boldly and emptied it in one go. It was a wild scene that the lady of the one-night stand subsequently played out: she made it clear that he had not only drunk water mixed with a cleansing solution, but that he had swallowed her contact lenses, and she demanded their speedy return. For a while after that, at difficult entries in pieces he was playing in, he was in fear of the lenses either coming back up and stopping his breath, or causing trouble in his bowels. From now on he frequented hotel bars instead of strange beds.

Ursula knows the names behind innumerable stories of the nomadic life of the orchestral musicians. Behind those stories there might not have been many great secrets. Discretion was a significant reason for Ursula's success, but it did not stop her from taking part in the fun of 'her children'; yet she had to steer clear of anything that could hurt feelings, constantly keeping in mind what was below the belt.

About Benjamin Britten too there were many rumours whispered over many a fence behind raised hands, planted in strangers' gardens and fed with the manure of the green-eyed monster.

Regarding strangers' gardens, Ursula much preferred to throw those symbolic stones back over the fences, showing her goodwill; at any rate, to repay like with like and make absolutely sure that only anything positive was exchanged.

Benjamin Britten already knew Ursula vaguely from Lucerne. Paul Sacher, who was virtually Ursula's godfather, was in charge of the serenades at the Lion Monument during the Lucerne Festival. These serenades were one of the social highlights of Lucerne's musical summer, also known worldwide for their artistic value. Every year Paul Sacher chose a new work. Benjamin Britten contributed the *Serenade for Tenor, Horn and Strings*. The tenor was, of course, Peter Pears, the horn player Dennis Brain, who would later play the organ at Ursula's and Philip's wedding in the Church of St Bartholomew the Great. At a later performance of the Britten *Serenade* at the Lucerne Festival, a horn player from Zurich played the solo. Britten had incorporated some natural notes, which to the substitute horn player sounded 'wrong'. Paul Sacher was conducting and gave in to the player's wish not to play them. Ursula was annoyed at the way conductor and soloist had violated the composer's work and would have liked to have made her displeasure known at this embarrassment. Ursula was and is a fervent admirer of Benjamin Britten. His music is her idea of artistic beauty. And what a man Peter Pears was, Britten's partner!

Many musicians are more or less apolitical people who only involuntarily sink to the depths of politics, and rather unwillingly follow up diametrically opposed opinions and convictions. In

Ursula's life too there was little room for discussion about the only correct world view. She preoccupied herself just as little with religion and questions of belief. Yet when Philip Jones had to live with the fact that his cancer would end in his death, Ursula and her husband managed in his final weeks to find the peace and calm to think and talk about their lives, which had often tended towards different directions yet were intensely interwoven, and to confront the Last Things without timidity and fear.

Benjamin Britten was a convinced pacifist and declared publicly that he would never dream of voting Conservative, and made no secret of his relationship with his partner, Peter Pears, or his tendency to depression.

Ursula, moulded by the social and political attitudes of her family, admired the great composer for his unshakeable single-mindedness. Yet, Uncle Hans Erni was a self-confessed Communist for a while, and the newly printed Swiss bank notes he had designed had to be pulped: a Communist, even if he was not one through and through, could not be the creator of the safest currency in the world.

In her parents' house there was a coming and a going of all who had rendered outstanding service to the international music world. The private receptions after the serenades at the Lion Monument were legendary and are all recorded in the family visitors' books, many illustrated by Hans Erni. But Benjamin Britten became aware of Ursula because, in a short time, she had made a name for herself with the Philharmonia Orchestra, certainly a name of note in influential musical circles. Britten's musicians for his opera group were largely recruited from players in the Goldsbrough Orchestra. For his chamber operas Britten needed five strings, five wind players, harp, piano and a variety of percussion. This combination together with the singers was billed as the English Opera Group.

When Ursula had convinced Quintin Ballardie to change the name of the Goldsbrough Orchestra, nothing else stood in the way of an intensive collaboration with Benjamin Britten, and the ECO became his resident orchestra at the Aldeburgh Festival. The little town of Aldeburgh on the east coast of Suffolk, and also the nearby village of Snape, where Benjamin Britten and Peter Pears bought the unique maltings and had them converted into the famous concert hall and opera house, became the summer residence of Ursula and her ECO. On the occasion of the Aldeburgh Festival of 1967, Snape Maltings Concert Hall was opened by Queen Elizabeth II. Two years later the building was gutted by fire, was rebuilt and was once again opened by H.M. The Queen, in 1970.

Even though Benjamin Britten was not the easiest of men, and everything had to be done his way, Ursula's memories of the great musician and composer are in every way positive. Britten appreciated the reliability of the ECO, which was for him simply Ursula Strebi (Ursula always used her maiden name until she left the ECO). A personal friendship? Ursula goes into raptures when she talks about the electric atmosphere of the Aldeburgh Festival, how she stood with her orchestra right in the forefront and was there when in Snape something new was premièred, when perhaps that part of the world interested in music held its breath for a short while. And when Ursula thinks about how she was one of the privileged few who were able to experience a première of a Britten opera, a Haydn or Schumann symphony conducted by Benjamin Britten, then she knows that the summers at Aldeburgh with Britten's music were among the great moments of her life.

Immediately the anecdotes are there again, the disappointments, which belonged to the giddying heights as much as the baton to a conductor. Musicians do not live with fewer highs and lows, rough places and plain, sayings, wisecracks and words of wisdom than, for instance, sailors, farmers or cashiers in the supermarket.

Once when Benjamin Britten saw a name he did not like on the orchestra list, the composer gave the ultimatum that either the replacement bassoonist should go, or he would lay down his baton. Even Ursula was not able to appease the angered maestro. There was nothing anyone could do about his decision, and Ursula set out to find a bassoonist who could save Benjamin Britten's work and performance. None of the usual players in London were available, and in desperation she contacted the bassoon professor at the Royal Academy of Music in London who had a young student available. His reputation went before him as an obstinate, uncouth genius and who, if necessary, would go along with anything eccentric that conductors wished. He also turned out to be an out-and-out cockney. At the first rehearsal with the composer conducting they had to stop because of a mistake by one of the string-players. When Benjamin Britten raised his baton again the bassoonist took the opportunity to point out an inconsistency in the score: 'Mr Britten, don't you think there is something wrong here in your score?'

Britten faltered, looked down at the score. Ursula froze and expected an outburst of unprecedented violence. Britten, however controversial he might have been in heterosexual society, was for all that the indisputable musical authority par excellence, while she, as orchestra manager, was only at the beginning of her career. How would he react? How would he judge her abilities? Could he trust someone who placed a young, inexperienced bassoon student in the orchestra, a player who exposed the great Britten, who, with his question, disputed his infallible mastery? Britten had the dignity to ignore the incredible cheek, or perhaps to accept the mistake in his score.

The Aldeburgh Festival was for the English Opera Group and the ECO one big success story. The relationship between Ursula and the composer was slightly strained when Britten engaged the London Symphony Orchestra for the recording of his opera *A Midsummer Night's Dream*, although the ECO had contributed a lot to the success of the acclaimed première. The LSO had clearly done a better lobbying job with Decca.

Ursula's ECO had already been ignored some time earlier, when Neville Marriner with his orchestra, The Academy of St Martin in the Fields, began causing a sensation and, as a member of the LSO, had better access to Decca. The fact that Neville Mariner, who was a friend of Ursula's, reaped the rewards of his recordings — not with fine sickles but with large scythes — yes, that did hurt, as Ursula readily admits, especially since the ECO was then probably the more eminent chamber orchestra and, with Britten, much more of a presence around the world on all the radio stations.

Ursula was and is an indefatigable doer, right into old age, and is constantly on journeys of discovery. Night after night, when no phone rings anymore, she sits at her computer, is connected to the world, spins her threads into a net that has to be so strong and tightly woven that, once they are on the list, all the young people will not fall through and be trapped in a no-man's land of insignificance. Her sphere of work nowadays no longer covers those who have made it. But she loves it when, at hundreds of events that turn her engagements diary into an impenetrable jungle, she meets artists, friends and colleagues of former times. Here she is warmly embraced by a great singer, or there a violinist, or a wind player from her ECO rushes up to her and brings back the times when they were best of friends with Daniel Barenboim, when Jacqueline du Pré, Janet Baker, Rostropovich, Zukerman, Richter, Perlman, Milstein and many others were one family.

'Do you remember that time in Saloniki when the hotel porter by mistake got Barenboim's passport muddled up with his father's; and his father had already set off for Athens on the night train? And the mix up was discovered in the middle of the night, the trains were alerted, and when they passed each other on an open stretch somewhere between Athens and Saloniki, the passports were swiftly exchanged?'

Or that time when Ursula was travelling with the English Opera Group in Russia, and, because of the samovar, particularly wanted to travel by train from Leningrad to Moscow but was forced to fly after all; and then, feeling rather desolate in a hotel in Moscow, came across a group of Swiss people from Sierre, and had a marvellous conversation with the pastor, the teacher, a wine merchant, while enjoying Fendant and other specialities from Valais that they had brought with them.

Lovely memories of events and occurrences, that perhaps happened a little differently, but at least more or less like that. Who cares? Ursula is always ready to indulge in reminiscences about the great summers in Aldeburgh, the world tours, the stories about the cultural and archaeological activities in their free time, to join in the loud laughter with suppressed wistful tears.

But more important is the young viola player who, with her partner, an equally highly talented violinist, is forming a duo, which is beginning to dominate the headlines in the feature articles of the press, just as the Tempest Flute Trio of the three phenomenal female flautists did. That is when Ursula's heart beats a little faster, she gets the itch: now it is worth staying up at night to work on their promotion.

When one is getting near 90 or even 100, it is sooner rather than later that time cannot be held up, if the evenings are not to end uneventfully.

It is a late rainy afternoon in November. The wind is blowing along the streets from all directions. Like huge snowflakes the leaves are falling off the trees and turning the pavements into slippery carpets. No dog should be chased out of the house in this sort of weather. In Kings Place, a relatively new cultural centre in Kings Cross, the ECO is giving a concert in honour of the recently deceased Sir Peter Maxwell Davies. Beforehand, at six in the evening, a film about the composer is being shown. Ursula was friends with Max, a person never ready to accept compromises when it came to music. (With whom was and is Ursula not acquainted?)

Ursula is working on a concert with top student brass ensembles of the major UK music colleges. 'A Celebration of Brass Chamber Music in Memory of Philip Jones': an event that she has organised in London every two years since 2013.

As is now almost normal for her, and being so engrossed in brass music ('Brass is my passion!'), she has lost track of the time. In order to catch the bus to Edgware Road tube station in time she needs to walk at a brisk, concentrated pace. Since her operation on a neck vertebra Ursula is not as safe on her legs as she used to be. It is early evening. There is a traffic jam. For a long time no bus comes. The rain is driving horizontally now. In the bus the passengers are packed in like sardines. Ursula would like to get into a conversation about the Prime Minister's Brexit plans but lets it go. She lives without a television, but listens eagerly to the BBC news on the radio, preferably on the dot of midnight. She knows the quickest way from the bus stop to the underground station from her days of teaching archaeology. Her steps become a bit quicker, although, as already mentioned, her feet seem to get further and further from her central nervous system. The Underground train is overheated. Although a younger woman wants to offer her a seat, to get through the tightly packed passengers is too difficult.

'In the old days,' says Ursula, 'people used to read the paper on the bus and the underground. Nowadays they are all staring at their smartphones and doubtless make typing errors when they are exchanging texts with their thousands of friends.'

At King's Cross the rain has let up a bit. To imagine the hurrying masses under umbrellas as well would be a nightmare. An endless queue of buses is barely moving forward at walking speed. On foot to Kings Place takes almost fifteen minutes. The road has to be crossed. Ursula sees a gap between the cars in the one direction, hurries to the middle, the traffic stops for a few seconds, a driver waves her over. It is another twenty to thirty paces to the cultural centre. It is ten past six. Ursula gains a couple of steps on the steep escalator down to the two concert halls. The film seems to have been late starting. There are still a couple of free seats.

A commentator standing in a bare, hilly landscape, talks about Peter Maxwell Davies's career. His music put people's backs up, was thought of by critics and a large section of the public as too difficult, incomprehensible and, to anyone with normal hearing, unbearable. But children loved experimenting with the young music teacher. On the Orkney Islands, far from disturbing influences, in a house without any creature comforts, he discovered melodies that sounded different even from the so-called modern music that occasionally came on the radio. His compositions got more and more visual. His fan club grew. He triumphed at the Proms. The Albert Hall cheered when he incorporated folk music in his symphonies and when, on the famously notorious Last Night, a bagpiper marched into the hall. The committed environmentalist with his social and often politically extreme views and uncomfortable music was named Master of the Queen's Music. No, he had not committed sacrilege by accepting this office of great honour. Perhaps the royal household did not entirely understand his music, but he and the Queen were like-minded as far as ecology was concerned.

Ursula is obviously proud to have valued and known Peter Maxwell Davies well in all his facets; also, always to have judged him correctly. With her mother she had experienced a performance of *Eight Songs for a Mad King*. The king, mad as he was, or at least had behaved, sat himself on a lavatory during the performance. He was not just pretending, as her appalled mother wanted to believe. Ursula was fascinated by the performance.

The concert following on from the film, with the conspicuously younger-looking ECO, drags on rather, due to a chatty commentary, never seeming to end. The last piece makes up for the long-windedness: *Farewell to Stromness*. That piece has to have been influenced by the Orkney Islands. Only recently Ursula played the piece on the Steinway piano in Philip's studio under the roof of her house in Hamilton Terrace, and decided to play on that beautiful instrument again more often. If only the feeling in her fingers, lost because of the neck operation, would come back.

In the Green Room of the Kings Place concert hall Ursula encounters the new artistic director of the ECO, the viola player, Lawrence Power. Another young man, Simon Crawford-Phillips, whom she once discovered with the Kungsbacka Piano Trio, is wild with joy at seeing Ursula again. The instrumentalists of the ECO she no longer knows. And how would she? In 1974 she passed the management on. That is over 40 years ago. During the conversations that immediately got going and in which the many young musicians enthusiastically included her, it almost seemed to Ursula as if these musicians were about to set off with her the next morning to the Aldeburgh Festival with Ben Britten and Peter Pears, just as her players had done in the past.

# Chapter 11

## *Concert Tours Seen from a Pre-Columbian Point of View*

Ursula always was a mountain climber, attracted by the Alps just as much as by the Andes, and later the Himalayas. Not to mention Kilimanjaro, which she climbed at 65. Philip gave her the flight to Nairobi as a birthday present. 'Get it out of your system!' It is exciting to hear her describe a thrilling concert, an opera that makes cold sweat run down your back but also induces euphoric happiness, and seeing her shed tears of laughter and emotion in her enthusiasm. Exactly in the same way she tells of climbing a 5,895-metre mountain that rises up out of the steppes of Africa into the sky like a pyramind, like the Tower of Babel. Breathless in the thin air. And the litter and excrement that people had left on their way up to the summit! As it said on the voucher, Ursula was paired up with her neighbour, Sherry, from Hamilton Terrace. All the male participants of the small tourist group gave up long before the top. Only she and her American neighbour made it to the summit of Uhuru Peak.

'And then you are standing up there. Really on the summit, and nearer to heaven than almost anywhere else in the world. You never want to come down again. Because in that sober mood you realise: now you have achieved what you wanted. Higher than this you cannot go.'

At that time, before the move into the 21st century, Ursula did not know that years later she would float down into valleys from other summits, if not quite as high, on a paraglider.

With the ECO she conquered one cultural peak after another; without getting out of breath but with the occasional cold sweat. On a world tour, when they were on the way from San Francisco to Australia, and before they celebrated a triumphant success in Sydney, there was a concert planned in a small Australian town for them to play themselves in, and play themselves out of their

116

jetlag. Ursula planned the performances very precisely and was valued by her musicians especially for her exactness to the last detail. For that reason it was all the more embarrassing when she discovered that, because of the date line, tomorrow would become yesterday. Thank God she realised the mistake in plenty of time before the orchestra set off.

With the talented pianist, Daniel Barenboim (who also set new standards with the ECO with his conducting), Jacqueline du Pré and other great musicians, her orchestra became an institution, the acronym ECO the ultimate seal of perfection. What could be achieved musically had been achieved.

Was she getting tired? Losing the zest for ever newer horizons? Sea voyages were not Ursula's thing, although the ECO did play on some exclusively musical Caribbean cruises. 'With firm ground beneath one's feet, there is less danger of taking off.'

Whenever she was travelling with her musicians, and if between her duties anything archaeological was within reach, she took the opportunity to satisfy that curiosity, that thirst for knowledge she had had since childhood. Deep inside her, there, where the unfulfilled wishes and the unexplained dreams were, something must once have been triggered.

No, Ursula Jones is not inclined to esoteric pipe dreams. That she got wiser with age could certainly be true, provided that wisdom is not equated with composure. More composed, more tranquil, satisfied with herself, the world and the things achieved, Ursula is not. Her energy, despite her widowhood and health problems, is unflagging.

If the four-thousanders can no longer be conquered on foot, or rather with artificial knee joints and a replaced neck vertebra, one can just float down in tandem with an experienced paraglider pilot from a somewhat lower mountain top; and, to mention just one of her engagements, to co-operate in Gerhard and Anna Pawlica's chamber music cycle in the Marianische Saal in Lucerne and, as always since 1996, in October to bring young musicians from England to Lucerne and to other concert venues. The list of artists reads more grippingly than any 'Who's Who'. It seems as if nothing more can go wrong if Ursula Jones begins to have faith in someone: from Daniel Barenboim and many others to the supremely good as well as glamorous star trumpeter Alison Balsom, the percussionist Colin Currie, the guitarist Miloš Karadaglić, the accordionist Ksenija Sidorova, and the composer and conductor Duncan Ward.

At that time, when the London Sinfonietta, with its much more modern repertoire, might have joined up with the ECO, Ursula could easily imagine that the combination of Britten's Opera Group, the young Sinfonietta and the ECO, could have resulted in the best chamber orchestra in the world. Quintin Ballardie, the co-owner of Ursula's brilliantly managed orchestra, waved it aside, and Ursula reflected on her husband's suggestion that, instead of exhausting herself for music, she should swap the latter for the auditorium. But Ursula cannot remember ever being exhausted; nor can anyone who knows her imagine it.

The rumour, that the rapid rise to success of the ECO might have made some players big-headed, that they had enjoyed their status as world stars too early on, did not survive for long. After 20 years in the war zone of the music business, Ursula was aware of her value and that of her protégés, for whom protection no longer seemed a priority. They would not so easily lose the seal of greatness that she had stamped on them. Whenever she meets current or long since retired members of the ECO, her charisma is always a topic of conversation, however much she tries to avoid it. Not that she would be praised to the heights: it was too long ago for that now. But the belief that the orchestra was then absolutely unique, moreover closely connected to Benjamin Britten, Daniel Barenboim and Raymond Leppard, has lasted over two generations. A golden age: Daniel Barenboim for the classical and romantic repertoire; Benjamin Britten for the modern, contemporary; Raymond Leppard for the baroque.

'Probably, just like that time in Arth-Goldau, the points were switched for me just at the right moment: the lever was pulled into the correct position by a wise hand.'

If Ursula had not been a competent connoisseur of the constantly changing scene, one could talk of coincidences. However, whether Ursula believes in them is doubtful. She probably likes the idea of strokes of fate even less. 'It just turned out that way', one often hears her say. But she knows too, of course, that things did not simply happen by themselves: they had to be helped along. It did not need to be shouted from the rooftops that every change of direction in her life was always on her own initiative. She rang up Philip Jones, wanting to engage him. He said no, and she did not give up. 'Because I was convinced that he was exactly the trumpeter that I still needed for Verdi's *Requiem*: the best.'

How disappointed she was when she had the opportunity to introduce her new husband to the great Otto Klemperer, and the maestro asked what role the man had to play in music, whereupon Ursula proudly replied:

'Principal trumpet in the Royal Philharmonic Orchestra.'

'A very bad orchestra!'

Another one of those, Ursula thought, horrified and close to tears. He conjures up out of orchestras the best interpretations of immortal works of the greatest composers, and stands there, trumpeting insulting phrases out into the world. Later, during his time as principal trumpet in the Philharmonia Orchestra, Philip Jones and Otto Klemperer became good friends.

The grand seigneur, Kurt Stavenhagen, was quite a different matter. Ursula came across him on a concert tour in Mexico. Self taught, with a prodigious collection of pre-Columbian art and cultural objects; a learned person who was interested in anything offered to him from the time before European influence, who collected everything, did not ask the value or price, relying entirely on his knowledge and his infallible instinct. Ursula fell in love with the treasures of that time, that already as a schoolgirl she had wanted to research. But then she had given in to her parents, who had persuaded her that she would not be able to afford a decent living by digging up fragments from ruins: broken jars, coins covered in verdigris and rust.

What was it about the history of the ancient world, the highly acclaimed western world? Surely for her this new, unknown world was at least as interesting as the battles of the Swiss confederates against the Habsburgs and Burgundians, which had been drummed into her. She could not get on with them at all, anymore than with the Thirty Years or the Hundred Years War. But she likes to remember the history lessons that were about the building styles: Gothic, Renaissance, Baroque, Art Deco, Roman, Greek, and those of even older peoples.

Mr Stavenhagen became Ursula's pre-Columbian mentor. It was unbelievable what he knew, what he could talk about. Hanging on his lips, always learning new secrets, being allowed to witness when mysteries were being solved; Ursula felt that she was being gripped by an enthusiasm similar to the time when she began living her music adventure. She had grown up with music, had got to know the great interpreters, the conductors and composers, in the flats and houses of her parents. Her understanding was sharpened, her senses reacted to everything she heard, and she became aware of what stood out above the average, what would endure, what would be forgotten.

All these experiences that she had, without having to do much herself, were an advantage when she began as a maid of all work with the Philharmonia Orchestra, and the people around her soon noticed that they had a natural talent on their hands, who could also speak languages that the English, with their global language, did not often need to.

With the history of the New World, with everything that there was still to dig up, that talent would behave differently. What Ursula gleaned from Kurt Stavenhagen on the craziest car journeys of her life, both fascinated and confused her.

'It was as if I was driving in a film. The pictures dazzled me. I wanted to hold onto them, put them in order. But barely seen they were already gone again, and other even more impressive and fantastic ones replaced them. Mr Stavenhagen drove with his car through history in such a way that I sent quick prayers into the sky shimmering in the heat. On the one hand I wanted to escape the mad traffic in Mexico City unscathed, on the other I wanted to make sure that all that I saw, in Kurt Stavenhagen's collection, in the museums, and the excavated evidence of a stunning culture, was not a dream.'

Thus it became ever more necessary to consider Philip Jones' proposal, to say goodbye to the ECO, to sign up for the Faculty for Latin American Studies, Institute of Archaeology, University of London. Already in her forties she knew it would not be easy to keep up with young things of around 20, nor to sit down and make the decision to swap the exciting life of a successful orchestra manager for concentration on a science which would necessitate meticulous procedures with shovels and brushes.

Moreover, Philip was on the way to success with his ensemble and to making history. The specialist world pricked up its ears to hear what trumpets, trombones, a horn and a tuba were capable of. The gifted players, inspired by their mission, only needed someone who knew how to market their enthusiasm; although they were all standing on their own two feet in a life of music and perhaps should have known better. Yet they believed that the world should at last be made aware of the music that they could blow out of their instruments: anything that people seemed to think sounded better coming out of stringed or woodwind instruments, out of harps and pianos, as the composer had written it, could be played on brass. Over centuries they had treated their ears to the composers' orchestrations. But nobody fills a concert hall without an impresario, without someone who knows how to awaken the public's interest; even with tricks that no one need be ashamed of.

Ursula imagined that as an archaeology student without the hectic work of managing a chamber orchestra that performed worldwide, she would have the time to promote her husband and his colleagues to the Hall of Fame. Promote: an important concept in show business. How was music, even the serious kind, different from a show that wants to be heard, seen, celebrated from mouth to mouth, from ear to ear?

Nobody could imagine Ursula having a comfortable, unhurried life, one without being constantly to hand and in demand. At the university she joined up with the legions of students, who were accustomed to quite a different rhythm from that of the woman who could well have been their mother. Here was the manager with an endless circle of acquaintances and friends, the globe-trotter, ready for any eventuality, the freelance worker with no security, and fending for herself; and there were the young people, who admittedly had chosen an area of study but were still very ambivalent about their aims, most of them on firm ground, with parents or authorities who had made it their duty to guarantee the financing of the next few years. Young women and men for whom studying was easy after their training at secondary school, who had discarded the ballast and could now concentrate on the essentials and had much free time to look for partners of whichever sex. They could commit to the most diverse political beliefs, throw wild parties, doggedly participate in sports and, above all, heard and played completely different music from that which Ursula, even without her ECO, Philharmonia Orchestra, Britten, Barenboim, du Pré, Zukerman, had ringing in her ears, as well as what she heard her husband playing on the trumpet.

Ursula, loving human contact, always curious about anything new, and firmly determined to stay on top wherever possible, soon got the hang of things, learnt quickly how to distinguish what was important and what one could ignore in the lectures and seminars, how one approached exams, and what made the lecturers, assistants and professors tick. She liked the university way of teaching and learning, and she had her studies basically under control, as she did her orchestras and musicians. 'One can of worms is like any other.' Apart from the languages and commercial practice, the general knowledge acquired with her business qualification at the Commercial School for Girls had got rather lost over the years and had to be dug up again, like the shards of Roman settlements on building sites in London that she had to bring to light (in every case on a prescribed quadrat), wash, list scientifically, document, analyse and describe in essays.

Apart from that, her commitment to the Philip Jones Brass Ensemble became ever more demanding but, without the amount of travelling that the ECO had involved, there was enough time left to get engrossed in this new field. Ursula describes her time at the University of London as very balanced, peaceful, but in every way highly stimulating. Now one might call it happily taking up the reins again of a once learnt metier, rather as it is for mothers who, after years with their children, try to get back to the time when they had been forced to give up their lofty aims, only temporarily, as people said in encouragement, and as they too persuaded themselves.

Ursula's wish for children was not fulfilled. That the ECO was her child: well, the orchestra was not a complete substitute, but seen over many years, and when she meets the now ageing musicians from those days, the comparison does not seem so inappropriate. The ECO was her child, not her substitute child.

Ursula is not very keen on metaphorical parallels. She does not like to mourn over a loss and tearfully look for something else: a new rose bush, to plant where the old one can no longer bud after a cold winter.

Looking through her photo albums she sometimes becomes thoughtful. The memories are wonderfully arranged according to her private and professional lives. Many pictures have yellowed, many are without a caption. What is obvious is the love and care taken in the arrangement. Up to the year 1999 all is in a systematic order. After that the photos are partly still in files, envelopes, or boxes. With Philip's illness the sorting into order of many common interests was no longer important. And it is unlikely that she will ever manage to sit down on her Persian carpet in her wonderful living room, pull the boxes and files off the bookshelves, spread out the photos on the floor and extend the system into the new millenium. Her last archaeological trips to Central America and the cultural tours that she led, have been recorded by others digitally, organised with commentary in Photoshop and Design-Programm. 'Like professional but perhaps less personal photo albums.' In every holiday group nowadays, however small, there is always at least one participant who will take on the work that, in the past, led to the famously notorious evening slide shows.

Philip's death caused a break. Ursula no longer dared to pursue with great personal creativity something that she could no longer share with her husband. It would have been too upsetting.

Ursula is not too embarrassed to dissolve into tears if, in a concert or opera, the trumpets take over and remind her of Philip's brilliant playing. If in the theatre or cinema something emotional is going on, she will be in unrestrained sympathy either with the suffering or the joy. But kitschy feelings she distinguishes with absolute certainty from genuine emotions. She did not consider the film, of a true story about a drug-addicted street musician with a stray cat, worth watching until the young man was suffering frightful withdrawal symptoms, battling with death, in front of his wide-eyed cat.

Also, when three attractive, young female flautists, the Tempest Flute Trio, turn up in Hamilton Terrace and take over the house, Ursula finds herself in a strange, emotional dichotomy. She is very happy to see the three artists again whom she has discovered and promoted. She even made possible and organised a very successful Swiss tour. But she is saddened that the trio were not taken on by the Young Classical Artists Trust, and she cannot understand it. Competition among young, talented musicians is immense. Whoever finally achieves the status of 'outstanding' depends more and more on chance as well. Ursula thinks about what could now be done, who could offer them similar opportunities to YCAT, who could guarantee the necessary connections, not just start them off, which the Tempest Flute Trio no longer needs. The flautists accept the elimination with a relaxed and sporting attitude: 'We lost in the final.' Next year they will get another chance.

Ursula does not comment on it. A silent uncertainty is perceptible. To let things run their course seems not to be a bad option. Perhaps the young people have a relaxed attitude to failure. Ursula knows the YCAT people very well. Many of her protégés were under their wing. Some of the most successful artists have become ambassadors for the Trust, trying to enlist support from potential sponsors, and encourage rising stars to apply to YCAT. It can be achieved with great talent and an iron will to practise untiringly, practise and practise again and, once in with YCAT, doors open to what one is then allowed to dream of. Without dreams there is no way in through the stage door.

The Tempest Flute Trio have not come to Hamilton Terrace by chance. They have brought their instruments, sheet music, stands and professional recording equipment in rucksacks, bags and cases. Helen has arranged several numbers from *West Side Story* for flutes and piccolo, and been shown the green light by a label. First the musicians want to ask Ursula's opinion. Not about financial support. For once money does not play a role; not an essential or decisive one, corrects Holly.

When *West Side Story* created a sensation in the London West End, and Bernstein's musical broke all records and filled the cash tills, Ursula was in charge of the orchestra, was the fixer whose responsibility it was that the music was played every evening and at every matinée, that the musicians were there on time and were just as punctually paid, and that the rigorous union rules were adhered to. Who, therefore, was more suited, if not the midwife of those timeless melodies, to test the idea of reducing the orchestra to three flutes, and to judge the songs, underlain with trills, tonguing, the clatter of keys, smacking of lips and heel tapping.

'I feel pretty', 'Maria' and 'Somewhere' are planned for today. Ursula lets them play the arrangements to her. Rehearsal nerves, the tension is like then, when the original was being rehearsed. Ursula feels as if transported back to those times. Young again. The Philharmonia Orchestra, the ECO, Benjamin Britten's English Opera Group, the Philip Jones Brass Ensemble. The enthusiasm one had to fire up, keeping the musicians in the right mood, no laissez-faire; smoothing things over if there were any disagreements in the orchestra; getting the conductor's passport swapped back on the open railway tracks.

With the reminiscences of a time that is as foreign to the three flautists as Facebook and Twitter are to Ursula, the nervousness of the flautists disappears almost completely. Yes, Ursula knew him, the great maestro with the furrowed face, the creator of *West Side Story*, the great Mahler interpreter, who also happened to precipitate one of the first crises in Ursula's and Philip's marriage.

Ursula was and is an admirer of Gustav Mahler and Anton Bruckner. Their symphonies got right under her skin and struck her right in the heart. When, together with Philip in the old Kunsthaus in Lucerne, she experienced all these emotions and snuggled up to her husband in a performance of Bruckner's Seventh Symphony, she did not immediately notice his scepticism towards this particular performance. Outside in front of the concert hall Philip took Ursula abruptly to task, as if giving an ultimatum, wanting to know if she could seriously warm to that vulgar interpretation of Karajan's.

'What do you mean, warm to? Shivers of joy ran hot and cold down my back.'

Philip shook his head in horror. His whole stance displayed total contempt. Had he known that she would be enraptured by such vulgar schmaltz, such pie and mash gone wrong, he would not have contemplated the marriage twice, he would not have contemplated it at all.

Ursula's dumbfoundedness was even more genuine than Philip's eruption. Were they, who both lived with and through music, on two completely different tacks? Had she, after all, chosen the wrong way all those years ago in Arth-Goldau?

Not long after this sobering discovery Bernstein was conducting Mahler's second symphony at the Edinburgh Festival. As a precaution she gave one of the two tickets she had bought for herself and Philip to her good friend, the oboist Heinz Holliger, thus avoiding a further clash of temperaments. After the concert she and Heinz Holliger went to see Bernstein in the Green Room. Completely drained, with his collar unbuttoned, Bernstein was sitting with legs outstretched in a leather armchair and, after his interpretation of the inspired masterwork, was again able to imagine a very close relationship to Mahler.

'I feel that I myself composed this work.'

'If Philip Jones had been at my side instead of Heinz Holliger, the divorce would only have been a matter of time.'

The recording of the *West Side Story* flute medley works out well. The Tempest girls extend an invitation to an exclusive lunchtime concert à la Wigmore Hall. A low November sun shines through the tall windows in Ursula's living room, with art and books, a collection of precious archaeological objects and a square piano. The three flautists also dance; the sun casts a spell over the room, which they turn into a stage. Their version of *West Side Story* would certainly have pleased Lenny Bernstein.

And Hundertwasser would not have spared his compliments either. Hundertwasser?

This name means nothing to the young women. On the walls of the generously proportioned living room hangs a series of ten works in strong colours glittering with gold and silver by the great Austrian artist, Friedensreich Hundertwasser, who also worked in the field of environmental protection. On a German tour with the ECO in the late 1960s Ursula discovered the numbered Hundertwasser series *Regentag (Rainy Day)* in a gallery in Stuttgart. As a passionate art lover she did not hesitate for long, advanced herself the orchestra's fee, bought the silkscreen prints and brought them home to London with the orchestra's luggage. Philip was on a foreign tour with his ensemble. Ursula had each work expertly framed and then hung in the living room. 'With Hundertwasser our house acquired a counterbalance to the graphics of Hans Erni.'

In this, Ursula had not reckoned with her husband. When he returned from his successful tour, told her in the kitchen about the concerts and the responses of the audiences to his chamber music, Ursula did have rather an uneasy feeling about the altered living room. What if he reacted, as he had done before to Bruckner and Mahler, to the gaudy colours, the glitter, the unconventional, in no way rounded-off Erni-like shapes, to the radical environmental themes?

Philip was no typical brass player, no beer-swiller like some of his colleagues, who often lacked any understanding for art and culture. With an extremely fine awareness, he engaged in anything that demanded an alert mind and intellect. But unlike Ursula's, his curiosity had its limits. Also, as an Englishman, or rather a Welshman, he considered his home to be his castle. First and foremost he wanted to feel well and protected at home, to enjoy a bit of peace, and he would not tolerate any bustling activity that went against his established rhythm, that could drive him out of his comfort zone.

Philip stopped short. There was already too much art in the house. Uncle Hans on all the walls. He had learnt to cope with that. He had also consented to the artistic creations by Uncle Paul and Aunt Berti. When, halfway up to his wardrobes in the bedroom, he walked into the living room and the loud colours, the childish figures, the wild butterflies, the fabulous creatures, the moon faces, ships and whatever other monsters, screamed at him from the shiny metal frames, embraced him with gestures, wanting to draw him in, he rushed out onto the staircase, supported himself with one hand on one wall and with the other on the opposite wall, almost lost his senses and shouted for his wife.

Ursula thought that she had expected anything, even him mocking her sense for art, but not this almost hysterical outburst.

'You've ruined my house with this rubbish!'

'My house,' he said. At least half the house belonged to her too.

'Hundertwasser!' The name alone spoke volumes. And Friedensreich to boot. *Rainy Day*. Dark colours. Opposer of straight lines. A madman who took his biological latrine with him on journeys, and took pleasure in the natural decomposition of his excrement. No. Never. Philip refused to enter that completely disfigured room ever again.

It was a worse crisis than an earlier one, when Ursula, despite his urgent pleading, was not prepared to give up smoking. But the Hundertwasser pictures stayed on the walls. Ursula was convinced that, with the then controversial art, she had given the house a creative boost equal to any contemporary work written for her ECO or for Philip Jones. Philip played works by Henze, Rautavaara, Lutoslawski with his ensemble. Hundertwasser somehow fitted into the same category.

Stubborn: like mother, like daughter, thought Philip and gradually became accustomed to *Regentag* in the living room, and if one did not pay too much attention to this weird Austrian, he would hardly place his loo, half-filled with turf, under the big pear tree in the garden, causing the neighbours to demand more insistently that his wife undergo an irrevocable change of lifestyle.

Without 'ifs' or 'buts' Philip was proud of Ursula's Bachelor of Arts degree that she acquired in 1978 after three years at the Institute of Archaeology of London University. Now he did not only have a renowned manager in the music business as a wife, she had now proved that her interest in this pre-Columbian 'rubbish' was not just a quirk. Ursula began to teach, to lecture, and what he heard about her from her audiences and colleagues confirmed his observation that his wife really was a phenomenon. He himself was not much help, when she asked him to give her his opinion of her meticulously prepared lessons, readings, lectures and seminars. When she tried out her lectures on him, she often found that he had fallen asleep. Not so when she was preparing his tours. He played all round the world, performing with his ensemble. Vicious tongues maintained that everywhere

where Ursula suspected or was reliably informed that the local museums housed relics of the pre-Columbian age of Central America with which she could widen her knowledge, the PJBE had had longer breaks after their concerts, or the tours had even been planned with archaeological interests in mind.

When Philip Jones announced to his ensemble after a concert that he would herewith end his active career, Ursula saw that her time had come to crown her academic ambition with a doctorate. Philip could have become Head of Music at the newly founded Music Academy in Hong Kong, and Ursula had the opportunity to take over the running of the Hong Kong Festival. Great was the temptation for her to organise sensations in the Crown colony as, in the past, with the ECO and Daniel Barenboim. Philip hesitated, and rather saw himself in London and as an ambassador for the brass chamber music he had promoted. When a top person asked him if he would take over the directorship of Trinity College of Music, he did not hesitate long and made the decision to give of his knowledge and ability in his own country, to invest in the education of young talents, and give Ursula the green light to continue her archaeological studies. The theme of her dissertation resulted from her knowledge of the pre-Hispanic artefacts in Central America. The British Museum, with its unique collections, became her second living room and study.

In the late 1980s owning a computer was not yet a matter of course. By means of an intensive one-day course she picked up word processing, and more or less got the hang of creating documents. A considerably younger cousin and godson was already a computer specialist and guided his godmother into the world of databases. Ursula began to feed her computer hundreds if not thousands of pre-Columbian grinding stones of Central America, especially decorated ones, and added innumerable details. The system fascinated her more and more. New bits of knowledge, lucky findings, surprising discoveries left her astounded. She had been bitten by research: the science became a passion.

In music management it was all about having a talent for organising, about her preparedness to react to the unexpected, to human and all too human problems, so that no one came to any harm. She had to make sure that the right sheet music was on the right music stands, that Benjamin Britten did not have the wrong bassoonist sitting in the orchestra, that, when on tour, Anita Lasker-Wallfisch was never confronted with nightmares about Auschwitz, that the homosexuality of some musicians did not lead to confrontation with the homophobic point of view of others. Now it was all about recording the tiniest ornaments, about placing prehistoric finds in location and time as precisely as possible. For the first time in her life Ursula had to be patient for hours, days or weeks, had really to allow herself time.

After his equally hectic life full of demanding performances, Philip Jones found great satisfaction in reorganising Trinity College. What to Ursula was the exact and thorough recording of her specialist objects was to Philip his task on behalf of the hundreds of students and their teachers.

Ursula handed in her dissertation at the beginning of 1992. In the summer of that year she gained her PhD in Archaeology. She was 60 years old. Proud? Well, a bit, admittedly. Philip too. If he had not given up active trumpet playing until a later date, which could have been quite possible, she probably would never have had the chance to start something completely different again, and make the best of it.

That time of meticulous research also did her temperament good. No mid-life crisis. No bitterness about having missed the right moment and seen her dream and its realisation get ever further away, year after year.

It was like when a friend told her that after he had been to a fortieth birthday party for the twelfth time, he was definitely never again going to sing along with same-aged people in the whiny song *Ramona*. Why *Ramona*? Because it had been the sentimental hit song of those 40-year-olds. *Ramona* at twenty, *Ramona* again at forty because the twenty years in between had not sufficed to get out of life what should have been. *Ramona*, because after forty, nothing works properly anymore. Did her good mood stay with Ursula because she never had time to sing *Ramona*?

At 89 Ursula still sits at her computer, feeds it with data relating to the day's activities, her almost incalculable undertakings. The dependence on this monster, this all-achieving apparatus, seems to occupy her noticeably more.

During a conversation about good or strained relations with neighbours, Ursula mentions that when the phone once rang at midnight, she did not think anything terrible had happened and picked up the receiver quite calmly, assuming that Duncan Ward, who was conducting abroad, wanted to let her know how the concert had gone. But it was the neighbour, recently moved in next door, who curtly demanded that she turn off, or at least turn down, the television. Ursula did not understand her spitefulness and said that there must be some kind of mix up, misunderstanding or a wrong number, since she did not possess a television. The neighbour, who had always had a dead pan face even if she entered or left her house at the same time as Ursula left hers, and the two were only separated by railings, now really let rip before slamming the phone down. Only then did Ursula realise that every evening at midnight the radio in her bedroom automatically came on. The detailed BBC news is Ursula's most important contact with political and other happenings in the world. As she is often still somewhere else in the house at that time, the radio actually is set at quite a high volume. What is more, it is standing on a chest of drawers against the wall of the house next door. But it was always there, and the Johnsons, the previous neighbours, with whom she was and is great friends, never complained. The noise insulation in the house itself is not particularly good. But the dividing walls are thick enough not to make noise-sensitive souls see red. Oh dear. In the morning at seven the radio was programmed to turn itself on too.

Ursula made the decision to apologise, in case the neighbour really was forced to listen to the detailed BBC news as well. The tiresome matter could not be resolved and the neighbour could not grasp the fact that some people could still manage without a television. When, on top of that, the keyboard of her computer got into a muddle and at first with cautious, then with increasingly violent prodding still would not work, the dispute with the unapproachable neighbour, unusually for her, did get her down somewhat. She even allowed one or two unaccustomed words to pass her lips.

'I have no time for television, and in newspapers there is more advertising than news. If my radio starts being objectionable and the computer plays havoc with me, I suppose I shall just have to begin to accept that I am gradually getting too old for all this stuff.'

The ill feeling did not last for long. If the Rolex Oyster had also functioned as a stopwatch, then between the switching on to measure the bad mood and the switching off at the end of it, the hand would hardly have moved.

'Whoever needs a stopwatch, does not have control over time.'

# Chapter 12

## *Ursula and the Fourth King from the East*

Philip Jones was for many years on the jury for the prize-giving at the renowned Royal Overseas League Music Competition. Every year this institution, which is active in the whole of the Commonwealth, gives considerable sums of money to young musicians and artists. And every year Ursula donates a prize for the best brass player in memory of Philip. The great ROSL final in 2016 was won by the Australian violinist, Emily Sun. Had she been on the jury, Ursula would also have voted for her. The fact that the winner of the wind and brass section left empty-handed might have made her a little sad. The reputation of the gleaming instruments and their players is constantly improving since Philip Jones's unceasing efforts, and today no trombonist, horn player, tuba player or trumpeter is ever laughed at anymore if he enters competitions with the strings, pianists, singers, oboists, percussionists, clarinettists, saxophonists and flautists. Yet they still remain somewhat in the shade of those instruments: those that one does not need, occasionally, to control with mutes. It was therefore astonishing and unique that a bass trombonist, James Buckle, was awarded the ROSL gold medal in 2017 against the winners of the singing, piano and strings categories, and acquired £12,000 in prize money. In 2019 another trombonist, Kris Garfitt, won the gold medal too.

Ursula is an honorary member of the ROSL and thus takes the opportunity to offer accommodation in the beautiful clubhouse on Green Park to participants of the culture trips she organises: a haven of peace and rest in the centre of London after a packed programme.

Night after night Ursula works through all her tasks as guide through the metropolis of music and visual art. She does not leave anything to chance. Having received so many letters thanking her for unique experiences, she wants, each time, to offer even more that is exclusive, authentic, and not what one normally gets on trips to London. Assuming that the interest is there.

Ursula sometimes returns home to Hamilton Terrace still feeling a little hungry, after her almost daily visits to evening events in the concert halls and theatres of London. Then she might like to sit down to a plate of spaghetti, turn a piece of toast into a delicacy, prepare a fruit cocktail, look forward to cheeses and grapes, to drinking a glass of wine and finally, together with her strong espresso, allowing herself a little glass of Baselbieter Kirsch. Then is the time to go over the evening in her mind, glance at her agenda and to discover that tomorrow, the next days, weeks and months are so booked up that it will be difficult to experience anything unexpected.

'Oh well, somehow I should be able to accept an invitation to dinner as well, not to miss *King Lear* at the Globe Theatre, and to experience the young rising star, the baritone Benjamin Appl (Dietrich Fischer-Dieskau's last pupil) in the Wigmore Hall.'

Even if there are undoubtedly differences in quality, Ursula salutes all achievements, is very sparing with negative criticism, counters vigorously if unqualified people find fault with artists. Constructive, sound criticism does no harm; but when people in certain circles just pull someone to pieces in the interval to make themselves sound clever, Ursula is capable of losing her usually polite self control, and making her opinion, her professional assessment, vehemently known.

One of her young musicians climbed the steep career ladder seemingly effortlessly, enjoyed the increasingly illustrious performances, the CD recordings, the exclusive record contracts, the euphoric reviews, becoming one of the musical jet set.

'Oh yes, that does happen. And that whole superficial glamour almost inevitably has an effect on the artistic standard of many rising stars.'

Not so with one of Ursula's protégés. The status of this prominent, good-looking artist could do him little harm. But then his muscles suddenly stopped playing ball. He began to have pain. After medical checks complete rest and a specialist therapy were prescribed. After the cancellation of several concerts and the concomitant journeys there was a sigh of relief. He was all right again. And then not after all. His body rebelled again. This worried Ursula more than it did the young musician. Had he taken on too much? Was there more to it than excessive physical strain? After another cancelled concert he poured his heart out to the person who had discovered and promoted him. There was something going on inside the young musician that could only be cleared up by means of a long conversation: not like the sort of kitchen talk that few were able to celebrate, ritualise and enjoy as Ursula did. By candlelight, the door open to the dining room with the original William Hogarth engravings of *The Rake's Progress*, Ursula listened to the young musician and, thanks to her almost inexhaustible contacts, helped him to find the right therapist. As a long-standing member of the board of the Musicians Benevolent Fund (MBF), a charitable institution that obtains professional help for musicians in need, Ursula knows how seriously an illness, an injury, a failing of the voice, a death, a divorce or a personal catastrophe can affect an artist, especially since few artists are permanently employed, and provision in old age looks anything but assured. The Queen was patron of the MBF (now Help Musicians UK) and usually present at the annual concert: a charity event with a big gala and high-powered sponsors. At the concert with the City of Birmingham Symphony Orchestra under the direction of Sir Charles Mackerras Ursula met the Queen and, during their conversation, was impressed by Her Majesty's profound knowledge of the tasks of the MBF. Ursula personally met the Queen several times.

Another charitable institution concentrates exclusively on supporting young musicians: Awards for Young Musicians (AYM), which Ursula supports actively. The organisation helps in cases where gifted young people lack the money for adequate training. Ursula tells of a talented coloured boy for whom AYM bought a piano and who now, much to the pride of his mother, gets up at five every morning to practise before leaving for school.

In the trendy restaurant Sarastro in Covent Garden there were some quite different encounters about which she still likes to talk. Richard, or 'King Richard', the owner, who unfortunately died far too young, who had a lot of time for opera, artists, marginalised people and those on whom he could rely, already doted on Ursula after her first visit to his atmospheric restaurant. The food was never anything special, but the owner was a likeable person, and his staff were of such infectious friendliness that even the greatest gourmand forgave him if what landed on his plate was not quite up to standard. Sarastro was, however, of a high standard where music was concerned. During Richard's lifetime nothing could be heard over the good and very loud speakers except opera. On some evenings there were live performances: young singers, 'the rising stars of the Royal Opera House', would visit the restaurant and, at some stage, spontaneously start singing to the guests.

Whether everything in Richard's restaurant, with its snugs and 'chambres séparées', was built according to regulation, can justifiably be doubted. Some of his guests were members of authorities, and the officers of the famous Covent Garden police station were among Richard's favourite customers. When the restaurant was fitted out in a building belonging to the Crown and, over a long period of time, was turned into a 'cultural' bazaar, the well known owner of the Prince of Wales pub by the Freemasons' temple went every day on a fitness walk with her Rottweiler. She was curious about the development of this other 'temple' in Covent Garden, but did not dare to take a better look beyond the threshold. Richard also became aware of the lady with the big dog. One day in Covent Garden Market he bought himself a wooden dachshund on wheels. Its tail was connected to the rather eccentric wheels and wagged even when the dog was no longer being pulled along on its lead. Just as the owner of the Prince of Wales passed by, Richard walked out of his door and spoke to the lady, having found out that she not only ran one of the oldest pubs but also an association of publicans. Might she, who certainly owned a more valuable dog than his and had had it for longer, give him some advice? Lady Barbara looked disconcertedly at the wooden toy dog, which was being sniffed over by her Rottweiler. She nodded. Could she recommend a cure for the worms that had obviously taken over his Fido's insides? Lady Barbara turned away without a 'goodbye' and made her way down towards the Thames. As if by order, two bobbies who happened to be known to her came around the next corner. Lady Barbara made straight for the policemen and asked them if they knew the mad Turk up there, the one with the wooden dog. What made her think the dog was wooden? the constables asked: they were reliably informed that Fido was a purebred German dachshund; the poor animal had for some time been suffering from parasitical worms, and his owner was very worried. Richard's humour appealed to Lady Barbara, who also had a few tales to tell about her fur coat: in a lift in the Rockefeller Centre in New York she was asked by an uptight animal-rights activist if she knew how many animals had had to lose their lives for her coat. Barbara posed a counter question: whether she, the young woman, could imagine how many men she had had to lie down with for this expensive garment.

Very soon Lady Barbara and King Richard became the best of friends.

Ursula's stories about Richard go back to an encounter with dustmen who every evening at midnight collected the refuse from Sarastro and, because of their reliability were also generously catered for every night by Richard. One evening when Ursula walked into Sarastro after a visit to the opera, she was shown by Richard to the table where the dustmen were sitting, and soon an excited conversation was underway. Ursula was interested in the work of the men, and the men liked all the different things that the lady from St John's Wood did. Richard put in a word too, telling them about all the people who became world stars thanks to Ursula, did not exaggerate in the slightest, of course, simply embellished a bit à la turque, and again told the world that Mozart and Verdi had been Ottomans, and if Ursula were a lady of the seraglio, he would single-handedly seduce her to the music of Mozart. One of the dustmen reacted to the name of Aldeburgh, saying he knew the best fish-and-chip shop on the entire east coast there, and also that out of the former maltings a concert hall had been built where the works of a so-called Ben Britten were performed in a festival every year. No, he had never been to a concert. But had she, Madame Ursula, ever been to the said festival?

'Why should I not divulge to my new, if somewhat unaccustomed friends, that I was an essential part of the Aldeburgh Festival, that with my orchestra Benjamin Britten trusted me to produce the quality which became the yardstick for his music?'

One after the other the dustmen stood up, doffed their company caps, bowed before Ursula, as one would in front of a lady with such a life story.

King Richard subsequently told his guests from the Royal Opera House that the lady who was involved in the première of Britten's *A Midsummer Night's Dream* had often been off working with the dustmen and that, after a few tentative attempts, had cheekily sat herself at the wheel and had steered the heavy vehicles through even the narrowest of alleys. It was no good Ursula correcting Richard's boundless exaggerations. Anyone who with two new knee joints and a replaced neck vertebra could still learn to tap dance, climb the Matterhorn and paraglide from the summit, could also be trusted with a London dust cart without a second thought.

How could anyone doubt it? According to King Richard, Ursula Jones was the granddaughter of George Bernard Shaw, close friend of Toscanini and Sir Simon Rattle, conqueror of Kilimanjaro, soon off to Mount Everest, daughter of a mother who lived to be 107, and trailblazer for Benjamin Britten; Ursula Jones was the woman who handed the conductor's baton to the pianist Daniel Barenboim, has a right to drive a flock of sheep over London Bridge as a Freeman of the City of London, is a decorated Doctor of Archaeology and researcher of thousands of decorated pre-Columbian grinding stones, discoverer and promoter of innumerable talents who made it to stardom, sparring partner of Alex Hurricane Higgins, fastest cyclist in London, keeper of a piggy bank filled with black-cab fares, widow of the trumpeter of St John's Wood, disinherited heiress to a Swiss fortune, selfless writer of a will regarding an honestly earned fortune.

Ursula Jones, the somewhat sober Londoner with deeply rooted Swiss moral standards, knows how to handle Richard's imagination grounded in the Ottoman Empire: with laughter. And her friends from all walks of life know better than she does that King Richard, with his patina over the truth, is more than a little right.

But who was this Alex Hurricane Higgins? Alex Higgins was a snooker player from Belfast; snooker an English way of playing billiards. As in a royal drama the balls are allocated positions on a big, green baize table: the monarch is the black ball. It is worth seven points. The extras are 15 red balls forming a horizontal pyramid. Each is only worth one point, but there are a lot of them. At the apex of the wedge-shaped red phalanx the pink ball presents itself. The proud lady in pink is very conscious of her six points. Rather lonely in the middle of the wide green swathe, the blue ball waits for a chance to use its five points where necessary and as best it can. Lined up in military formation are the yellow, the green and the brown balls ready to award two, three or four points if the blue, pink and black are not ready to join in. Last but not least the white ball. Although materially of no value, nothing can happen without it: there would be no dialogue in the improvised dramas on the green cloth. It is the producer's cue: it is what gets the game going. Only at his command do the coloured balls start touching one another, sometimes tenderly like a kiss, sometimes clashing violently, frequently bouncing noisily off the edges, covering the most astonishing angles and pathways backwards and forwards on the table, hiding themselves cunningly behind each other, gloatingly depriving the key player of the click-clicking of points. They dance a crude polka when a waltz, a minuet or a pas de deux would have been called for; save themselves, when no feint helps anymore, in one of the six pockets, from which they return to the table, as long as there is still a red ball as surety for them.

Alex Higgins came into the spotlight out of the smoke-filled back rooms of Irish public houses, with their mighty baize-covered tables and coloured balls. He became the most brilliant player, the enfant terrible, the devilish loser and winner. The actor Richard Dormer wrote the play, 'Hurricane', about the gigantic (in the truest meaning of the word) highs and lows of his fellow countryman whom he greatly admired, and then acted the one-man show himself. The wildly acclaimed première in Belfast was followed by equally well-received performances, from the West End to Broadway. The play is a shattering one-to-one representation of the extreme life of a man who won millions and gambled away even more millions, was very popular, admired and never laughed at, mocked or despised, even after his wildest, most chaotic escapades. The actor and playwright acted just as 'crazily' as the original. The stage was a huge snooker table on which Alex Higgins's genius, inner conflict, his tendency to manic-depression, his excesses, his sarcastic humour and his often drunken misery became, from frame to frame, a complete work of art. Often it was almost intolerably realistic, only then to take off into spheres that made every member of the audience elated or deeply unhappy. Alex Higgins attended many performances, followed his alter ego from Belfast to Edinburgh, Sheffield and London; at the première he stormed onto the stage. His admirers in the audience cheered, and he acknowledged Richard Dormer's achievement with the words: 'You've got balls, son!'

Ursula saw a performance in the London West End. She had never before seen a snooker match, and had no interest in a sport that lasted hours or even days: 'Where was I supposed to find the time to sit for hours in front of the television and watch two men in waistcoats and bow ties around a huge table making life difficult for themselves with a few coloured balls?'

The play was so intense that Dormer fell into a 14-hour sleep after every performance. Ursula might actually have left the theatre a bit more shattered than the other red-eyed members of the audience. It took her a long time to drag herself away from Hurricane Higgins, this 'holy sinner', even though she knew of enough similar fates, if not as extreme. With hers and Philip Jones's commitment to the Musicians Benevolent Fund she got to know people who, between rejoicing to high heaven and plunging to the depths of despair, won everything and then lost even more. Alex Hurricane Higgins was once a slave to many women, who lost the ability to distinguish between the stage and real life, who spent money as if he were a Spanish king or a Russian tsar. The Northern Irish snooker hero could have been the violinist addicted to pills, the trombonist living beyond his means in an expensive house, the solo cellist who got multiple sclerosis, or a harpist now an invalid because of a road traffic accident of which she was guilty. They all and many more were suffering anonymously, could not shout out their misery from a stage like Hurricane Higgins, tell of their debts that they would never be able to repay, and, for shame, hardly dared to go on stage or into the orchestra pit again.

Ursula could not write a play and certainly not take over the leading role herself. She laughed at herself with the thought that even under the greatest strain she would not have needed as much sleep as the man who waved a cue around, like a magic wand à la Harry Potter, and with magic tricks despatched the coloured balls into the pockets at the table's edges. What she could do, however, was to listen carefully, look, and decide where and how she could help. The fund's money should be targeted as carefully as possible at those who genuinely needed it, without pillorying people for their indiscretions, but also without giving the impression of encouraging them through generosity, not lessening the importance of personal responsibility.

Ursula later followed a big snooker match in the Crucible Theatre in Sheffield. Because Shakespeare was also performed to the highest standard in this same theatre, it seemed to her as if she really was sitting in a theatre, and the coloured balls were the protagonists of a royal drama. It was neither Hurricane Higgins nor the almost as legendary Jimmy White who were duelling as producers. It was just a single player who, for a whole frame, was alone at the table, while his opponent, with stony expression and as if in disgrace, sat far from the action in a comfortable armchair. Ronnie O'Sullivan, following in the footsteps of Alex Higgins, despatched all the red balls to the pockets, and after every red one the black one too. After that he sank the yellow, the green, the brown, the blue, the pink and, right at the end, the black. He was credited 147 points: the absolute maximum. Ursula could tell from the cheering of the audience and the euphoria of the commentators what an achievement this was, and she searched for equivalents in music, literature, art. Yes, they existed, the winners of competitions; but not after a concert, a reading, a theatre production, the opening of an art exhibition. She did not wish to compare winning the Nobel Prize with a triumph in the world football championships or at the Crucible Theatre. And Wimbledon, Lord's Cricket Ground, the rugby stadium at Twickenham? Is there immortality in sport? In the United Kingdom is there a sports star who gets anywhere near the fame of a Benjamin Britten? Even if the Beatles or the Rolling Stones did not celebrate their successes on the same stages as the large and smaller world orchestras of Great Britain, their music is undoubtedly surviving far longer than high achievements in sport, and can always be heard again today, from long, long ago; much further back than the reports of sports results and records.

For Ursula there is no obvious common ground between music and sport, except that the same application and endurance is needed for high achievement in music and the other fine arts, as well as in sport.

In Soho the winner of the jazz prize of The Musicians' Company, a double bass player, gave a concert in a trio with a percussionist and a pianist. Pizza Express was the venue. The audience sitting at the dining tables was not run of the mill. At classical concerts and at the opera Ursula is more likely to encounter slightly greying people, and even at prize-winner concerts in the Wigmore Hall young people are not in the majority, but with jazz one would expect more of them.

'The youngsters are off somewhere else again,' an elderly lady on the next table comments. 'Somewhere where our already worn-out ear drums can only vibrate a little and can't process the sounds of the young anymore. Where you have to stand endlessly in a crowd waving lights to and fro, until your legs start aching and no one can hear you when you groan along with the hammering basses.'

In Soho, not far from the legendary Ronnie Scott's, there really are more elderly guests than used to attend such concerts. The jazz is a bit dated too, and with it the men who now tie their once shoulder-length manes into narrow, stylish ponytails resting on their shirt collars. Strange that one can so easily distinguish the audience of a concert given by the Philharmonia Orchestra from one of a jam session in Pizza Express by Hyde Park Corner or in Soho.

'It only applies to men,' the lady on the next table adds. 'We women can keep ourselves separate from our dreams and wishes much more easily, and don't cling to appearances.'

Ursula agrees with the lady. She remembers the music scholar who, at the box office, was amazed when he was told that it was all right to wear a T-shirt and jeans, even at a charity concert attended by a high up Member of the Court.

'As long as they are clean and they have washed their feet,' the lady insists, who is letting the rhythm of the jazz trio turn her into a seated dancer.

Philip Jones would gladly have played jazz too, and would certainly have played it just as well as baroque music. But, for reasons of perfection, he had his priorities; and there simply was not enough time for everything. But he loved going to Ronnie Scott's.

He was often off touring with his ensemble. A propos of that, Ursula tells the story of an hours-long jam on a German motorway. She was at the wheel of a VW minibus. It was hot. All the windows were rolled down or pushed back. John Fletcher took hold of his tuba, began to play a few notes, improvised whatever he could think of in that rather unpleasant situation. Probably the endless queues, in front, at the back and alongside, reminded him of Hans Werner Henze's *Essay on Pigs*. Philip put his trumpet to his lips and took over what John Fletcher had begun. It is doubtful whether Henze was the right composer to dispel the increasing nervousness, to steer the here and there audible irritation in a more conciliatory direction. Scott Joplin sounded more entertaining. Whether the Germans, stuck in their cars, could make much of 'Music for the Kings and Queens of England', was also uncertain. Paul McCartney's album *Tug of War* perhaps? There were no hooting protesters. Would a Sousa march please? A sequence by Gabrieli? A passage from Handel's *Water Music*? A bit out of Mussorgsky's *Pictures at an Exhibition*? A couple of lollipops? A concert for fellow-sufferers stuck in a traffic jam and people nervous about missing appointments. A resounding success, performed with joy. Without feedback? Absolutely not: when the queues started moving again, a joyful, long-lasting hooting concert got going. How could one tell that it was joyful? A car hooter as a rule does not show emotions: if anything aggressive ones. But rhythm: the joyfulness was made quite clear by that.

Philip Jones never got to experience the heyday of Sarastro, that establishment on the verge of kitsch. King Richard would have got him to play a signal from the Royal Box right across the room gleaming with trumpet gold and imitation glitter. Just as Shirley Bassey did not need persuading to sing *Goldfinger* to him and gave him *My Way* as a present, all that time ago when he could no longer stand after his last whiskey.

Once when Ursula had brought friends from her youth, of the best Lucerne society, to Sarastro, she was waiting until after midnight for her dustmen friends. When these greeted her exuberantly with 'Hello, dearest Ursula', the ladies, all dressed up to the nines, were somewhat surprised at the sort of people their little Ursula knew: not quite one's everyday friends. If things had gone her parents' way, she would likely have had to marry a man who later became the husband of one of these astonished friends, considered a successfully negotiated catch.

At a memorial celebration for the deceased King Richard, 'Sir David', for many years the loyal and helpful factotum of the restaurant, sang *My Way* in place of Shirley Bassey, who was otherwise engaged. Ursula would have liked to have joined in. Her voice, strangled by grief, would not let her.

# Chapter 13

## *OBE, Badge of Honour and a Chair Man*

For most of her life Ursula stood on many stages, but always left them when the curtain was about to go up. She left the footlights for others, not because she would be afraid of them, but because she was and is the manager in the background. She is the person with the extraordinary instinct for talent and what can be made of it.

'Sitting in the audience and being convinced that up there on the platform a young woman, a young man, almost still a boy, or a trio is playing, making the people in the hall catch their breath: oh yes, those are the great moments, when goose flesh creeps up your arms and, at the applause, tears pour down your cheeks. But that is little help to the celebrated artists if I don't go to the Green Room and meet them eye to eye, happy but exhausted as they are, and ask them about their career, about their connections with agents; and then offer myself as their lobbyist.'

Ursula does not actually like the term lobbyist. She does not represent interests, or groups of people who have them. Helper syndrome? Heavens, no! Ursula has no diminished feeling of self worth, which psychology ascribes to those who, almost like an illness, want to help everyone, and even insist on helping when it is not necessary. Never has she forced help onto someone just to make herself feel good or better. If she needed help herself she would take it unreservedly. Perhaps an arm that she can take after a long day in the office, after endless phone calls, writing dozens of e-mails; or on her way home, after a long evening on an uncomfortable seat unkind to her knees, though in an admittedly beautiful London theatre with hundreds of people keen on culture and entertainment.

Perhaps now and again Ursula considers her physical limits as of negligible importance, puts her own needs and wishes after

145

those of her acquaintances and friends. But then she soon remembers how satisfying and cheering her last trip to Mexico was, for instance, and how much she is looking forward to the olive harvest with dear friends in the south of France. And she will remember how happy she is to undertake an arduous journey to a concert given by one of her promoted artists, how much she likes the spaghetti prepared for her along with a glass of wine, when she comes home after a journey, rather more tired than a year ago. However, it would never occur to her to expect gratitude for having taken on, completely as a matter of course, something for the sake of someone else. Sometimes she is even a bit embarrassed by the way the Iranian family in her little coach house, with nice little surprises and culinary delicacies, show their gratitude for her accommodation regarding their rent, which could have been horrendously high, being in St John's Wood. But because she knows that her pleasure gives her tenants courage in their insecure situation, it suits her natural warm-heartedness perfectly.

When a letter then arrives one day from Buckingham Palace, Ursula thinks it must be an invitation to some sort of royal dinner, and already wonders, if she were asked to bring someone with her, whom she could ask to be there to give her an arm in case she tripped on those wide stairs. So she is all the more surprised to find that it is quite a different kind of invitation. It is the same kind that Philip had received twice, when she had accompanied him with fully justified pride. On the way to the great event she had had to promise her husband, in view of the importance of the audience, to refrain from personal questions or remarks, as once with regard to the Queen of Tonga, and to watch her tongue if the relationship with Lily Langtry happened to come up, as it had done once before.

But now it was she, Ursula Jones, who was to be named Officer of the Order of the British Empire (OBE): for her services to music. And over all those years she had not shied away from emphasizing her basically democratic views and, whenever possible, fulfilling her duties as a Swiss citizen. She often let herself be advised by visitors from Switzerland if she was not fully informed about a referendum. Inherently Swiss liberal, she discovered, looking back, that her advisors, mostly from artistic circles, had informed her in a rather divergent way; the small world of Swiss democracy had therefore never been seriously disturbed.

Ursula accepted the award with pride and satisfaction, without much fuss. There was no big party, but she was glad that there were seemingly enough influential people who considered her worthy of the honour. Whether the OBE after her name will be of any use, she will neither confirm nor deny. 'If I had to look for a flat beyond a certain category, I would probably have a better chance.' She barely ever mentions her Doctor title.

Ursula does not need a flat. She will stay in her house as long as in any way possible: in St John's Wood, in Hamilton Terrace, where an OBE is not so very remarkable. A green plaque hangs to the left of the simple brown wooden door, and shows passers-by and visitors that from 1964 until 2000 Philip Jones lived there: a great musician with two royal decorations. At number 10 Sir Charles Mackerras CH, AC, CBE was at home. His plaque is bright blue. It was Ursula and Philip who had alerted the Australian conductor to the fact that the house had come up for sale.

Charles Mackerras was the chief conductor of the Hamburg Opera and had a guest performance in London. His trouser braces had been left behind in Hamburg. The maestro asked Philip who was playing in the orchestra if he could help him out with this embarrassment. When Mrs Mackerras brought the lent braces back with thanks, she mentioned that her husband had been appointed chief conductor at Sadler's Wells Opera and the family were urgently looking for a house in London. Philip liked to say in appropriate circles: 'I was glad to inform Mrs Mackerras that the house two doors away had just been put up for sale, and soon Charles 'Mackers' moved in with his family. They became very good neighbours. My braces were and remained ruined. Charles must have sweated so awfully while conducting that all the elasticity had gone.'

In his younger years Sir Charles was supposedly an extremely temperamental conductor, loud and often very impatient. More than just a few musicians supposedly suffered so severely from his vehement behaviour that their anxiety sweat must have manifested itself in the wear and tear of their braces. Sir Charles became noticeably calmer, more amicable, more tranquil with age: a conductor who was highly regarded by all great orchestras, and admired by musicians. He sweated right up to his last concert, and because he liked to greet his closest friends in the Green Room, already rid of his soaking wet shirt, he would embrace the one or the other congratulator so warmly, that all the sweat was transferred to them.

Ursula had her basement made into a small, cosy flat with a living room, bedroom, kitchen and bathroom. For a long time this had been her office, and for years after she had given up smoking, a thick layer of nicotine still lay on the shelves and her complete collection of programmes of ECO concerts. Down there, with direct access to the garden, Edite now lives, a petite, attractive, always cheerful Brazilian. She does a perfect job of cleaning in several private houses and the care home in St John's Wood. She also looks after Ursula's house and garden, as if the whole place were hers. No one has hands as nimble as Edite's, and if her English often hits the limits of her language abilities, a smile flits across her face, and her eyes shine as if she has just been chosen as the year's Samba Queen. Perhaps Edite might not quite have the green fingers of her predecessor in the basement, but she is a good hand at everything practical in this typical London town house with five floors, and a thousand and one memories of the golden times with Philip Jones.

Years ago Ursula had taken over the Italian Marina from her American neighbours and friends, Rob and Sherry Johnson. She was a trained nurse, lived with Sherry and Rob, worked in a nearby hospital and, instead of paying rent, kept the house and garden in superlative order. Marina was a very serious woman. But she could put on an extremely winning smile when spoken to by neighbours on both sides of the house while she was passionately doing her work in the garden. Why she then gave up her hospital job and started working as a cleaning lady in various houses, remained her secret. Marina got the reputation for being the Samaritan of Hamilton Terrace when she solicitously looked after an injured Mrs Mackerras: at a Berlin Philharmonic concert conducted with great success by her husband in the Philharmonie in Berlin, she had been knocked over by a heavy man who had lost his balance. She had to be taken to the Charité hospital with a broken hand and cracked ribs, but was the next day able to fly back home.

With the rampant increase in the percentage of elderly people in the pleasantly dilapidated street of artists, every effort was made to keep hold of Marina after the Johnsons had moved away. Ursula, made wiser by the experiences of her aged mother, took over Marina plus cat from the next-door house and installed her, also rent free, in her basement.

Something must have happened to the serious yet hitherto very friendly Italian woman. Her smiles disappeared. When she was to be seen working in the house and garden, the grim look about her mouth could not be overlooked. If Ursula brought home guests after concerts and countless other events, Marina complained about the unreasonable noise in the, admittedly, not very well insulated house. It was not very pleasant for Ursula, who tried to avoid conflict, and asked her guests to be considerate to the occupant of the basement. Imagining being at the mercy of Marina, 'if it ever gets that far', turned into a nightmarish troublesome time. And yet it had been Ursula who had seriously considered offering the Italian woman a lifelong right to live in her mews, when she more or less took Marina over from her neighbours, and half of Hamilton Terrace saw Marina's caring for Lady Mackerras after her accident in Berlin, as a stroke of luck.

Ursula came to a different decision. She wanted to convert the basement into a state-of-the-art flat, which meant that Marina and the cat, Nacho, would have to cope while the building works were going on. Marina absolutely refused, especially since Nacho could not be expected to tolerate the dust and smell of paint. Then the old cat died, and Ursula decided on a total renovation of the basement. For Marina this was unacceptable. Immediately she refused to engage in any conversation, and one day she simply disappeared without saying goodbye to Ursula.

That was a person who had lived for several years in the house, enjoyed the absolute trust of the owner, had access to all the rooms, had green fingers for the garden, did not tolerate dust that was more than two days old, cooked, not always the dishes that Ursula liked the smell of, lived as in a palace during the longer absences of the owner, and then placed under her arm the suitcase out of which she had exclusively lived, and disappeared forever. A psychologist who lived temporarily in the coach house and got to know Marina, suspected that the reason for her strange behaviour was a childhood trauma, probably sexual abuse. Ursula was amazed.

If Marina's tom cat got the urge to roam and in the morning did not turn up for his food before the Italian woman had to leave the house for work, the former nurse woke up half of St John's Wood with her hideous yelling for her four-legged creature. The woman in the basement became more and more distant, and seemed set on controlling and tyrannising the whole house.

Sometimes Marina seemed to Ursula like a character out of the Jerry Springer Show in the Cambridge Theatre in London, to which she was taken by a friend. It was wild and vulgar, an unparalleled chamber of horrors. Abnormal people of all types put aside all feelings of shame, and bombarded each other with verbal atrocities and unambiguously ambiguous gestures; everything presented with the greatest professionalism, with tap-dancing Ku-Klux-Klan hordes. Tremendous but, in the same measure, repulsive: bad taste cloaked in perfection. Ursula recommended *Jerry Springer: The Opera* to others and thereby rather put her foot in it. To make friends with dustmen, let herself be driven home in the Rolls-Royce Phantom Six of a Turkish-Cypriot restaurateur and teller of weird stories, like the Queen of Hamilton Terrace, yes; but to extol to the skies a musical in which not only the most revolting taste was revelled in, in which it virtually stank of blasphemy and obscenity, no. Ursula took it more calmly than her former dislike of *Struwwelpeter*, haunting the stage as *Shockheaded Peter*. Ursula can cope better with Theatre of the Absurd than with music performed without dedication or fire in the belly: 'Excuse me. If the violinists, the other strings, the woodwind and brass stay stuck on their stools with their tails hanging down to the floor like the lame wings of fat crows, then, for a cynical satire, I would prefer competently tap-dancing Ku Klux Klanners.'

Mr Whittle was hers and Philip's devoted handyman, the 80-year-old former decorator foreman at Scotland Yard who never came to work in Hamilton Terrace without a tie. With him she went as a birthday treat to the ABBA musical *Mamma Mia* and let herself be carried away by his fascination for the music of the chart toppers from Sweden.

'They know how to do drama, Mrs Ursula. They might even know better than your Beethoven and Britten that after a peaceful, soulful middle section a rousing finale has to follow. Waterloo!'

When on a plane to Switzerland, where Ursula was to be distinguished with The Badge of Honour of the City of Lucerne, and a fellow passenger got her into a conversation about Royal Ascot, Ursula mentioned, without any kind of superiority, that she had followed the action on the racecourse from the Royal Enclosure in company with the Swiss ambassador, the lady did not believe that she had had such an honour and, as a test, asked her about the colours of the Queen's hat and clothes. Dr Ursula Jones OBE replied correctly, down to the last detail.

Ursula did not impose herself on the Swiss Embassy in London. The cultural foundation in the Swiss canton of Zug, Landis & Gyr, with several little houses in the East End, began to engage itself, with much sacrifice and generous financial means, with the cultural exchange between Switzerland and England. But the embassy did not take due notice of it until the managing director of the foundation in Zug directed the attention of the relevant diplomats towards Ursula. She was the person who was more familiar than anyone else with the music scene of both countries. She became a member of the Swiss Cultural Fund in the UK. Up to a point, she decided on the direction in which the creative side of Switzerland should be regarded in England. At her suggestion, the Swiss Ambassador Award was created. Every year the Swiss Embassy awards young, exceptional soloists or a chamber music ensemble the prize of a concert in the Wigmore Hall. For a musician to have performed in this concert hall so renowned for chamber music, is something very special.

Ursula's resistance to extravagant prize-givings was much talked about. 'Do without the champagne and the all too delicious canapés, and put up the prize money instead.' Good for the artists, not appropriate for representative diplomacy.

In the Swiss church in Endell Street, Covent Garden, refurbished by Swiss architects Christ & Gantenbein, Ursula organised regular concerts with young musicians under the name of Swiss Connections. The sacred space is a jewel yet acoustically rather a disaster. But the church's congregation was looking for someone who was familiar with the music scene, had the necessary connections and knew how to get musicians, singers and the necessary audiences together. Who could that sought-after person be other than Ursula? But Ursula is not a church-goer. After the death of her husband and the impressively arranged funeral service in the church in St John's Wood on 26th January 2000, Ursula occasionally attended the Sunday services; largely because of the music and the above average choir. To Covent Garden she goes for the opera, for a concert and, until King Richard's death, to Sarastro. But that is in the evenings: during the day it is definitely too far to Endell Street.

Yet, in the end, she was committed to the concerts in the Swiss church, as she is for anything that she has said 'yes' to. 'If only it were easier for me to say 'no'; to say 'no' more often.'

The church congregation was not very co-operative. Ursula brought her friends and acquaintances along as voluntary helpers. The successful businessman who offered to help set out the chairs for the concerts and to put them away again, is neither a church-goer nor a Swiss, but proud to be Ursula's 'Chair Man'. From experience Ursula knows that flyers and church newsletters only recruit a few older members of the congregation. For every concert she wrote hundreds of personal letters and e-mails. So as not to carry too far the frustration of the loyal helpers and the musicians dismayed by the impossible acoustics, she would have preferred to throw in the towel; although admittedly, having the best fish-and-chips restaurant in London in the same street made it a prime venue.

For a long time Ursula has been on the board of trustees of the Lucerne Festival, is a board member of Streetwise Opera and the National Youth Wind Orchestra of Great Britain, sits on the board of trustees of the Samuel Gardner Memorial Trust, for the preservation of public trees, gardens and footpaths, and for the promotion of the arts and musical education; she is President of the Maria und Walter Strebi-Erni Trust in Lucerne, board member of a trust dedicated to promoting musical exchanges between India and the United Kingdom, member of the Royal Society of Musicians, and member of the Park Lane Group, which promotes young musicians. She is a Freeman of the City of London, honorary member of the Royal Northern College of Music and honorary life member of the Royal Overseas League.

All these honorary memberships, the decorations for her services she could consider as the reward for her indefatigable engagement in all things, her commitment to support and promote those institutions, a reward for her now to enjoy with pride. But she would not be Ursula Jones if all she did was to go to the annual general meetings, board meetings and illustrious dinners. In her engagements diary, planned for a year ahead, they crop up all the time: the funds, trusts, boards and societies. She is a 'feared' meeting attendee, always as well prepared as possible, armed with dossiers, argumentative when there is a question of keeping the administrative costs down for the sake of the promotion funds. The fact that, in the course of her duties, which she does not take lightly, she often turns up at meetings a little later than scheduled, is sometimes mentioned in the minutes, but mostly tolerated with much understanding, and usually with a smile.

Since she has her new knee joints, a neck vertebra operated on in the Nottwil Paraplegic Centre, and a temporary paralysis in her toes and fingers, and can no longer run after red buses and race down escalators in the underground, she allows more time for her journeys, much to the joy of her fellow trustees, members and friends; also, if the distance is too great, goes without her bicycle. 'Since, thanks to my Freedom Pass, I no longer need a taxi, I certainly don't want to have to start paying the congestion charge.'

None of her friends have any idea whether notoriously fast cyclists like Ursula have to pay the congestion charge. If at her age, on her three-gear bike, often loaded with shopping, she were still ever to flit past cars, taxis, lorries and buses, one could expect anything of the mayors: from Ken Livingstone, via Boris Johnson to Sadiq Khan.

'You've missed something,' is one of her stock comments. Most of her friends and acquaintances suffer from a modicum of bewilderment. No one can work out how Ursula manages, more or less, to stick to her timetable. Yes, one could understand it if she were to arrive at appointments in a rush, unprepared and not quite immersed enough in the matters at hand; if, the next day, she no longer knew what she had done, heard and seen yesterday or that morning, what people in her circle had missed. She might no longer be able to tell in detail the story of an opera she has just seen, or she might have forgotten a number in the Deutsch or Köchel catalogue; but that she could confuse Tom Stoppard with Alan Bennett, or Alban Berg with Arnold Schönberg, or the Bruegels, not be able to tell budget from expenditure, or to distinguish precisely between the Mayas and the Aztecs: 'Well, old age hasn't got quite that far yet!' That she might occasionally drop off during concerts, in the theatre, at the opera or at committee meetings, when they get boring, she will certainly not deny.

Ursula goes into raptures when she talks about her membership of Streetwise Opera. She has nothing but admiration for the idea of leading homeless people back to a sheltered life by means of music. Ever since she got to know the dustmen in Covent Garden at close quarters and showed great respect for those night workers who dispose of our refuse, she looks quite differently upon circumstances, which, although she was aware of them before, did not have for her the significance that they deserved. Her musicians were also night workers after all.

Matt Peacock was an opera critic and did some work in a hostel for the homeless. A politician had written in the press about the many homeless surrounding the Royal Opera House Covent Garden and the English National Opera in St Martin's Lane. He had intimated how unpleasant it was for visitors to both opera houses after the sparkling performances constantly to be stumbling across the homeless outcasts of society, wrapped in their blankets and sleeping bags, covered with cardboard boxes. So Matt Peacock decided to concern himself with the condemned homeless, how to deal with their misery, whether self-inflicted or not, in a different way from that of the well-known relief organisations. He spoke to the people living on the streets and invited them to workshops with musicians, enthused them with opera, which was anything but elitist.

'No, it was no Sisyphean task. It was, it is work: hard work, gratifying work.' He was himself surprised at what his idea sparked off, not only with the homeless but with the people from whom he asked for money to realise his plans. In Westminster Abbey, the year 2002 saw their first production: it was the first complete performance of Benjamin Britten's *The Five Canticles*, with professional singers and musicians. Members of Streetwise Opera mimed the stories and enjoyed a sweeping success. *The Times* wrote that cynical commentaries in the run-up to the experiment had feared an amateur result. The same people frankly observed exactly the opposite: a deeply moving story of the highest musical standard was staged, or rather was performed, in the time-honoured abbey. Benjamin Britten, the composer of *The Five Canticles*, would have bowed deeply before these artists of quite another world.

Matt Peacock's work not only afforded the public and the press unexpected encounters and insights: many of the participants, unjustly described as people on the side lines, managed to re-enter society out of which they had, voluntarily or involuntarily, stepped or been pushed. With further highly praised productions, in New College Oxford, at the London Handel Festival, with the *Rückert-Lieder* in Nottingham, an opera in Newcastle, at the Almeida Opera Festival in London, with a video show in the Royal Festival Hall in London, a co-production with the Spitalfields Winter Festival, Streetwise Opera created sensations. At the event, *With One Voice*, homeless people of the United Kingdom sang with the Royal Opera House Covent Garden at the 2012 Olympic Games. A year later, homeless from all over the country again excelled in a wonderfully weird *The Answer to Everything* at the British Film Institute on the London South Bank. Another opportunity came when Streetwise Opera took part in all performances of the opera *Dialogue des Carmélites* by Francis Poulenc in the Royal Opera House, Covent

Garden. Sir Simon Rattle conducted it. Under the direction of Matt Peacock at the Olympic Games in Rio, the singers, lifted out of their misery, were celebrated enthusiastically. Streetwise Opera is not about being praised to the skies by the press and highest government authorities, even though recognition, praise, and permission to spread the idea can be very useful. Every single homeless person who recovers their sense of self-esteem, and who no longer avoids society, is more important than a page in *The Times*, in *The Guardian*, *The Telegraph* or a recording for broadcast by the BBC. Ursula Jones has been involved almost from the start, enlists potential donors among her friends and acquaintances, and provides ideas for composers.

'No concert, however perfect, no great opera, no epoch-making theatrical production can get anywhere near experiencing people who have given up all hope of being at home under a sound roof again, passionately taking part in a great project; seeing the faces of singers lighting up when their voices are heard in public venues, and the audience visibly moved.'

It was not Ursula's idea to help the homeless, whom she also repeatedly came across, especially near to the great cultural centres. But when she heard that more could be achieved with music than with kind words, blankets, soup, tea, soap and toothbrushes, with delicious left-over sandwiches from the City and not too terribly worn-out books from public libraries, she was enthusiastically onto it and discovered in Matt Peacock a unique personality that suited her own temperament and commitment. Ursula knows that, because of the way society works, there are more and more homeless people everywhere, despite Streetwise Opera. It cannot be denied that many people thus affected no longer wish to leave the streets. But if Matt Peacock and his helpers, by now grown into an impressive army worldwide, can with his projects motivate people to more confidence and a new start, then that is much more than a drop in the ocean. Philanthropy through action. There is, however, too much misery. On the streets of London and other cities it can be eased, without a grim declaration of war, by music.

# Chapter 14

## *"Là-haut sur la montagne"*

Over more than 60 years in the British Isles Ursula Jones became a Londoner and can no longer imagine living permanently anywhere else, not even Switzerland. Naturally she always has her red passport renewed. Probably she is also quite proud of having dual-nationality. Would she say she belonged more to one country than the other? As both countries are among the most stable of states, and she is hardly ever disappointed in either and is happy to belong in two places legally, she considers nationality simply as an ambivalent matter of feeling. Perhaps that was why she and her husband bought a chalet in the canton of Valais, above the Matter Valley near Zermatt. Ursula's mother advised them to entrust the surplus of the fees Philip earned outside England to her, for her to invest profitably. Although the purely personal relationship between son-in-law and mother-in-law was never quite free of conflict, the leader of the PJBE had, ungrudgingly, to admit to the skilful and lucky way Ursula's mother had with money. When Philip saw, after quite some time, the new value of his savings, he could barely believe it, and suspected machinations from which he might have to disassociate himself. His mother-in-law was amused by his doubts; Ursula just shrugged her shoulders. She simply could not understand the almost biblical increase in funds.

The chalet 'Chems' above St Niklaus was their only material possession in Switzerland. Small but all the lovelier, surrounded by firs, pines and larches. It was just as it should be: after leaving the city and travelling to Valais, there was the ride in the postbus, then walking through fields in full bloom, through the fragrant summer grass, autumn colours or, in winter, tramping through knee-deep snow to the sun-baked little chalet. Here Philip would play the alphorn with as much virtuosity as his trumpet. From

'Chems' he and Ursula went on unforgettable mountain walks, here they celebrated Swiss National Day with the villagers on 1st August, which was also their wedding anniversary. On New Year's Eve the New Year's singers came by: up there, where the trees rustled in the wind around the house as in Johanna Spyri's *Heidi*, where Ursula was nearer to heaven, or at least to the stars, where at full moon the summits of the Valais Alps turned into the backdrop of Benjamin Britten's *A Midsummer Night's Dream*. Here the trumpet and the alphorn echoed back from all directions, more quietly in a minor key if the original had been played in the major. Here was where Philip's ashes were scattered to the wind and earth, accompanied by the tones of 'Là-haut sur la montagne', played by his brass colleagues.

From then on, as a widow, Ursula undertook much more demanding mountain and climbing treks than those she and Philip had planned and done together. Perhaps rather foolishly, she climbed twice up to a rock face that, mistakenly, she thought she knew well, once with a woman friend and then another time alone and without safety equipment. A path on the edge of a sheer drop got ever narrower and unsafe. After a blind bend she came up against an insurmountable rock, and when she turned round to retrace her steps, the precipice made her shake with fear, for from this direction it looked far more threatening. Paralysed with terror, she could not take another step, neither forwards nor backwards. The fact that she had her mobile phone with her seemed like a miracle. Also, how she managed to make an emergency call on it, bordered on a mystery.

'Superb, how that helicopter came; a rescuer was let down on a rope, tied me to himself, and we were pulled up together through the violent downdraught of the rotor blades.'

No less spectacular was the flight to safety. At first she was a bit surprised that the mountain rescue was not free of charge, although it made perfect sense. But then she understood why the bill was so steep: it had not been an easy undertaking to get her out of that awkward location. On landing, her rescuer said: 'I'm sure I know you from somewhere.' A couple of years before, he had been her mountain guide on the 4,027-metre-high Allalinhorn.

With the automatic exchange of banking data and virtual lack of confidentiality, it became more difficult to possess properties in two countries. The tax authorities in Great Britain started helping themselves rigorously, and Ursula decided to sign her beloved chalet over to her godson and cousin, while keeping the legal right to live there until her death. It is understandable that she feels she had the right to live forever up there where, once inside the door, there are no appointments, no concerts, neither opera nor theatre, where no red buses must be run after, where there are no escalators down to tube stations, and cycling on the steep streets and paths is not an option. And no longer are there skis in the cellar waiting to be clipped onto somewhat worn out legs and feet. If it came to it, she could hire the new kind. Whether she could still stand on skis and 'wedel' down to the valley as she used to, or would experience the same fascination on the pistes as on a tandem paragliding flight, will have to be seen. In order not entirely to dash her hopes for a ski-comeback, she will wait for the time being, for modern skis might be developed exactly to suit her handicap. Could this reasoning already be the wishful philosophy of ageing, secretly held by many of her friends?

So is she worried about getting old? 'I'm old already!' she replies to such questions, which she says are stupid. She does not mention the Erni gene. That it might be somehow comforting that Aunt Berti made it to over 100, Uncle Hans to 106, and her mother to 107, Ursula does not want to dismiss out of hand, but preferably out of mind. Become dependent on helpers and carers? 'On no account.' Ursula has already laid plans.

And then there was also the house in Morcote. A jewel right by the lake. Her parents had had a unique opportunity to acquire the little house on Lake Lugano with its large terrace. Ursula's mother loved the house above all else. She had had it done up according to her needs and her unmistakeable taste by an interior designer and decorator, a stylist and great master of his trade. Well over 100 years old, she spent a lot of time in Morcote, looked after by loving staff; she took pleasure in the view across the lake to Italy. After Maria Strebi's death the house in Morcote was part of the estate to which Ursula no longer had any claim.

However, when Ursula took over the chairmanship of the Maria und Walter Strebi-Erni Trust she was then able to delay the sale of the real estate, so desired by other trustees: not out of self-interest. Nowhere can house concerts on a summer's evening be more beautiful than on that loggia, shielded by the wall from the noise of the street. The Trust demands a considerable amount of rent, which Ursula will pay for as long as she can.

The history of the house? Between the 16th or 17th and the 19th century rich Milanese built their summer residences in Morcote. Ursula thinks that the present-day Villa Melitta was a gardener's or servants' house. Before the Strebis, the owner was a certain Herr Scherrer, by trade Hitler's personal tailor. He was an art collector and creator of the Parco Scherrer, a park that he made over to the Morcote community. His wife was a dancer, and an admirer of the Amalienburg in Munich. Some of this admiration is evident in the house on the lake.

Philip gave Ursula a boat on receiving her doctorate. 'Not a yacht,' laughs Ursula, 'but it was a rowing boat appropriately christened Doktor Metate'. No, by then Ursula did not wish to live there forever either, should her energy no longer be equal to being constantly on the go with things musical. And again, no, she did not think that it had to do with the history of the house. Perhaps that earlier loss of inheritance played a role. And had it not been for the music that Miloš Karadaglić magicked across the lake with his guitar, or the sounds of all the young musicians that Ursula invited to Morcote, then the ownership situation would long since have changed again.

Disappointments? Yes. The thousand lives of Ursula Jones would definitely have run their course a little differently had it not been for one or the other non-fulfilment of her most heartfelt wishes. Ursula experienced her worst shock in Southwark Cathedral in London, when Bach's *Christmas Oratorio*, conducted by Benjamin Britten, was on the programme. The continuo player was not a member of the Musicians' Union. If he did not join the union, the other musicians were not allowed to play. Blackmail. The continuo player would not give in, Benjamin Britten and the whole orchestra were on his side. Even Ursula's husband, Philip, was not exempt from the playing ban. Of course

Ursula knew the Musicians' Union's rules but hoped that the presence of Benjamin Britten and Janet Baker would weaken the fronts. 'Yes, it seemed to me like war. And I lost.' The performance nevertheless took place. Britten conducted, the soloists and choir sang, the harpsichordist played the continuo, and the organist took on the orchestral music. The orchestra sat perplexed and dumbstruck on benches at the back of the cathedral.

Concerning her estate there will be no ignominious arguments. Her property, limited to the London home, she very wisely had valued by an independent, renowned agency. The house with garden, in one of the most sought after residential areas of London, is certainly worth something. What Ursula and her husband purchased is now worth at least three hundred times what it was. The proceeds will one day massively benefit institutions that have devoted themselves to music. The Royal Philharmonic Society will be in charge of the Philip and Ursula Jones Musicians Fund. The list of beneficiaries is long.

Ursula and Philip Jones will occupy a place of honour in the history of British music.

**Ursula Jones: dates**

Ursula Jones Ph. D., OBE, born 11.3.1932 in Lucerne

1939-51    Primary, secondary schools, and commercial school in Lucerne graduation

1951-53    School for Interpreters, University of Heidelberg, Diploma in Translation (German/French/Italian)

1953-54    School for Interpreters, University of Geneva Diploma in Translation (French/German/English)

1954-57    Orchestral secretary, Philharmonia Orchestra, London

1956    Marriage to Philip Jones (1928-2000) on 1st August

1958-59    Management, Goldsbrough Orchestra, London

1960-63    Founder and director, International Art Club Editions, London

1960-74    Co-founder and General Manager, English Chamber Orchestra, London

1975-78    University of London, Institute of Archaeology, Bachelor of Arts (Archaeology)

1975-86    Management, Philip Jones Brass Ensemble, London

1978-92    University of London, Institute of Archaeology Part-time studies (pre-Columbian Central America), Ph. D. (Archaeology)

1978-2000 Lecturer and teacher (adult courses): City University London, City Literary Institute London, British Museum, Westminster Adult Education, WEA etc.

Since 2000 After the death of Philip Jones, guest lectures in the UK and abroad on the subjects of Ancient Mexico, Philip Jones Brass Ensemble, climbing Kilimanjaro, supporting talented young musicians and organising concert tours for young musicians

*Board memberships*

Lucerne Festival
Streetwise Opera, London
National Youth Wind Orchestra of Great Britain
Samuel Gardner Memorial Trust, London
Maria und Walter Strebi-Erni Stiftung, Lucerne (President)

*Memberships*
Royal Society of Musicians, London
Worshipful Company of Musicians, London
Park Lane Group Advisory Council, London

*Awards*
Hon. Fellow of Trinity College London (2000), Freedom of the City of London (2003), OBE (2010), Hon. Member Royal Northern College of Music (2013), Hon. Life Membership Royal Overseas League (2014), Badge of Honour of the City of Lucerne (2014)

**Photograph copyrights**

The numbers refer to those of the photographs

© HM The Queen & BCA Film: 19

Ursula Jones, private collection: 2, 3, 4, 5, 6, 7, 8, 9, 10, 11, 12, 13, 14, 15, 16, 17, 20, 21, 22, 23, 24, 25

© Suzie Maeder: 1, cover photograph

© Royal Northern College of Music: 18

Printed in Great Britain
by Amazon